MAGA...
DR... ...ING ...
FABRIC LANDSCAPES ...
BEANBAG TOSS ...
BABY BOX-BUGGY ...

There's no such thing as "nothing to do" when you have *Free Family Fun* ... loaded with imaginative ideas for games, arts and crafts, family outings, and more!

Switch off the TV and discover real family fun—for free!

FREE FAMILY FUN

Berkley Books by Cynthia MacGregor

FREE* FAMILY FUN
(*and super cheap)

MOMMY, THERE'S NOTHING TO DO!

FREE FAMILY FUN

(AND SUPER-CHEAP)

CYNTHIA MacGREGOR

B

BERKLEY BOOKS, NEW YORK

FREE* FAMILY FUN
(*and super cheap)

A Berkley Book / published by arrangement with
the author

PRINTING HISTORY
Berkley edition / August 1994

ISBN: 0-425-14367-8

BERKLEY®
Berkley Books are published by The Berkley Publishing Group,
200 Madison Avenue, New York, New York 10016.
BERKLEY and the "B" design
are trademarks belonging to Berkley Publishing Corporation.

PRINTED IN THE UNITED STATES OF AMERICA

10 9 8 7 6 5 4 3

For the World's Greatest Mom
(otherwise known as Yvonne Epstein),
who always had faith in me,
taught me some of the games in this book,
and plays a pretty mean game of Geography

For Darla Brack,
best friend, ally, and aide

For Vic Bobb,
new friend,
whose help with my books is inestimable
and invaluable

Acknowledgments

The author wishes to thank the following people
for their contributions
(in alphabetical order):

Cathy Bobb
Vic Bobb
Sheryl Pease

Contents

✂ Introduction

"Mommy, will you buy me a new————?" "Daddy, I want a————." You've heard it often enough. You can fill in the blanks yourself. Whether the missing word is Nintendo or some other game or allegedly vital equipment for having fun, chances are you can't get it at the dime store. (For that matter, try to find a dime store these days—but that's another subject and another book.)

Today's kids don't know how to have fun inexpensively. They don't know about homemade toys and paper-and-pencil versions of games. They want the boxed version. They want the electronic version. In most cases, they don't even know there's an alternative. In many cases, their parents don't remember, either.

But *newer* and *better* aren't always synonymous. *More expensive* and *better* aren't always synonymous either. Sometimes something is better simply *because* it's less expensive or free. Economy is still a virtue. Now that we've put the acquisitive, easy-spend eighties behind us, maybe it's time to reclaim the games, toys, activities, and pastimes that amused us, our parents, and even previous generations without costing a parent's salary for a week. We can also invent new amusements for the nineties that are cost-conscious, preferably free.

Some of the activities described in this book cost nothing. They involve no materials whatsoever except brain power or imagination. Many more require only materials you already have around the house, such as pen and paper, or construction paper and scissors. Those that do require a trip to the store to purchase something won't bankrupt you on the outlay.

When I first set out to write this book, I conceived of it as a book comprised entirely of activities the whole family could participate in together. Most of the activities here do fit in that category, but I've broadened my scope to include some activities only suitable for older kids and their parents, or younger kids and their parents, or activities for kids that the parents are less likely to want to join in on.

I did this for several reasons. For one thing, you can't please all the people all the time, and not all family compositions are alike. Some families have only young kids; some have only teenagers, some have a wide range. Some families are comprised of one child and one parent, while others are five kids and two parents. An activity that's suited only to teens-and-older may *be* a whole-family activity for one family (Mom, Dad, and their only child, age 14) but not for the folks down the street with their three-year-old, eight-year-old, and twelve-year-old.

As for the activities that parents may not care to participate in, well, togetherness is a fine thing, but there are times when parents need to be off doing something else, and the kids should be content to play by themselves. The point is just to find something *affordable* for them to do. But the majority of activities in this book are suitable for the average family to participate in all together.

A fair number of the activities are educational, either directly or indirectly. Some of them teach outright; others just help to develop skills along the way. But I confess I didn't select them for their educational value. If you get an extra added benefit out of one of these activities, that's great, but I selected every one of them because it was fun or interesting. Education is important, but so is fun.

There are indoor and outdoor activities here, active and quiet, games and crafts, and family excursions, but all of them are free or very inexpensive, all of them are fun or interesting, and all of them are aimed at families, whatever their size and composition. Including yours.

Enjoy.

✁ Quiet Games
and Activities

ALPHABET STORIES

Materials needed: None

Although I've included this one in the "Quiet Activities" section, it, like some of the others in this section, can lead to some pretty loud laughter. It's suitable for any number of people from two up, but the more players the better. Almost any age can play except the littlest ones, and I am definitely including adults when I say "almost any age."

The game, which is noncompetitive and does not involve scoring or a winner, is as suited to car trips as to the living room. It's a great way to pass the time while the family is engaged in some chore together or out on a walk; just don't play it while you're drying the crystal serving bowl—someone's likely to get a fit of the giggles and—oops!

One player starts. It doesn't matter who, though you do want to keep the rotation the same as the game progresses. If Joanie starts the story, and it progresses to Mike, Mom, Vic, and Dad, completing the list of players, then it should keep following the same order as the game continues around again and again.

The player who starts sets things in motion with a sentence, preferably a silly one. It can be a piece of

5

dialogue ("Excuse me, is this where the giraffes are marching?" or "Unhand that possum, you traitor!") or a bit of narrative ("Donna had no idea why her hair had turned green," or "The twenty-one-story schoolhouse was the newest building on Mars,") or any other kind of sentence.

It is now the second player's turn. The second player must come up with a sentence that follows the first sentence logically to some degree, although it can be as goofy as desired, *and begins with the letter of the alphabet that follows the one with which the first sentence started.*

In the case of the sentence beginning "Excuse me. . . ." the first sentence started with *E*, so the second player must furnish a sentence that makes some sense within the context of the first sentence and starts with *F*. (Example: "Find a giraffe around here, and you'll win a pair of purple sweat socks.") In the case of the sentence beginning "The twenty-one-story. . . ." the next sentence would have to begin with *U*. ("Under normal conditions, Martian buildings were not allowed to exceed the height of structures on Venus.")

The third player must now come up with a sentence beginning with the next letter of the alphabet. ("Venusian buildings never exceed eighteen stories.") After the sentence beginning with *Z*, the next player must start with *A*. The game is over when play returns to the letter the game started with, which can be any letter in the alphabet.

Of course this is a silly game, played for fun and giggles, but in the process, the kids are stretching their imaginations, becoming more at ease with the alphabet (if they're still little and not totally sure what letter follows what), and even learning something about continuity and order in telling a story.

Variations for Older, More Sophisticated Players

Variation #1: Each player writes a situation down ahead of time, and all situations are thrown into a bowl or similar container. ("You're in a hardware store looking for radishes." "It's halftime at the Super Bowl and you've accidentally wandered into one team's locker room." "Your mom just announced that NASA has drafted her to lead the world's first exploration of Jupiter." "You're on an underwater exploration, digging into the earth's core.")

Now each player gets a turn to start a story, picking a situation out of the bowl. Again, the first player can start the story with a sentence beginning with any letter, but the others must follow alphabetically.

Variation #2: Players need not confine their contributions to a single sentence; players who wish to may carry the dialogue or narrative forward several sentences, though the first letter of the first sentence must conform to the alphabetical requirement.

GEOGRAPHY

Materials needed: None

Though this, too, is a great game for car trips, it, like many other car games that don't depend on license plates, billboards, or scenery you pass, is equally suitable for the doctor's or dentist's waiting room, or for any other occasion when you have restless kids, time to kill, and no materials handy.

If the kids have been studying geography in school, they may be almost as familiar with place names as you are, so this is a good game for parents and kids to play together, because age won't give you a huge advantage over the kids.

If they're weak in geography, this game will help

them get familiar with at least the names of various cities, states, countries, and continents. And if they have any curiosity at all about the unfamiliar and sometimes strange-sounding names they encounter in the game, now's your chance to drag out the atlas and familiarize them with the locations of these places.

The actual game is very simple: One player starts, coming up with any place name. The second player then has to come up with another place name that starts with the letter the first player's location *ended* with. (Example: If Mom says *Michigan*, Eric could then say *Nome*.) The third player then has to supply a place name beginning with the letter that *ended* the second player's offering. (Example: Since Eric said *Nome*, Linda could then say *England*.)

The game continues from player to player in order. When the last player has spoken, play reverts to the first player. No name may be used twice, not even if, for instance, there are two cities by that name, one in each of two different states or countries (Kansas City, Kansas, and Kansas City, Missouri; Paris, France, and Paris, Illinois).

When a player is stumped, and cannot think of a name beginning with the letter required that has not already been used, that player is out of the game. The last player left is the winner. Obviously, it is good strategy to try to stick the player after you with a difficult letter, by using a place name that ends in either a letter that doesn't begin many place names or one whose place names have largely been used up this game.

If, for instance, you are called upon to give a place name that begins with *G*, it is far more advantageous to counter with *Germany* than *Georgia*. Your kids will soon become familiar with such names as Ypsilanti and Yaphank, from hearing you use them when they stick *you* with a *Y*, even if they can't find these places on a map.

The number of people who can play can range from as few as two up to as many as you want.

One good thing about this game—besides its being both fun and educational, and a potential springboard to a later geography lesson ("Want to see where Ypsilanti actually is?")—is that the kids will quickly learn the names of many new places, making the youngest ones almost as proficient players as the older ones, and the older ones nearly as proficient as you.

ENCYCLOPEDIA SAFARI

Materials needed: Encyclopedia

There is no limit to this activity for two or more children, other than their attention spans. Each child chooses a volume of the encyclopedia at random and opens the book to a page at random, not too far toward the end of the volume. Each turns his or her own pages.

(A lot of indirect learning goes on when a child pages through a reference book: alphabetization skills are subtly improved, general familiarity with the encyclopedia becomes greater, familiarity with a variety of subjects increases, the child becomes more familiar with the use of headers and with the way a person gets oriented in a dictionary or encyclopedia, and unfamiliar words subtly make their way into the child's consciousness.)

When a player leafs through the pages and finally comes to an animal entry, he or she stops. When all players have animal entries before them, the kids have to each read something about their animal in order to determine whose animal is the largest. The one who has "captured" the largest animal wins the game.

For variety, other versions of the game can be devised. For instance, let the kids look for people, and the winner is the one with the person who was born first. Or let them find the person who lived the longest, which will involve math skills (subtracting the "born" date from the "died" date) as well as encyclopedia skills.

Geography can be invoked in looking for the farthest-south or farthest-north country. In fact, the items they can hunt for are limitless; the kids can even make up their own categories, once you've got them started playing.

Solo variation: The child plays alone, reading two volumes and betting on which book will win. Score one point for every correct guess.

DICE BASEBALL

Materials needed: Pair of dice, paper, and pen or pencil

This game is best suited for children and adults who are baseball fans and have a rudimentary knowledge of baseball scorekeeping. Many kids are knowledgeable enough about box scores to play at age ten; others may need to be a couple of years older. As far as upper age limits of players, the friend who contributed this game to this book pointed out that investigation of certain persons in their forties might suggest that the upper limit has yet to be discovered.

Basically a two-player game, it is also suitable for solo play in which one person simply determines the outcome of a match-up between two fantasy teams. Some people playing this game will want to use real Big League teams' and players' names for this, but most will find that it's a lot more fun to invent teams comprised of whatever real or imaginary people come to mind. One college professor who plays this game and shall here remain anonymous revealed that one of his starting lineups included Mickey Mouse, Joseph Stalin, Hillary Clinton, Darth Vader, Julius Caesar, the president of the college at which he teaches, Marv Throneberry, Dave Barry, and Arnold Ziffle (the pig on "Green Acres").

Play follows the rules of baseball, except that the outcome of each "pitch" is determined by the roll of the dice. If one player is playing, he is simply observing two fantasy teams, rolling the dice for both, and waiting to see what the outcome is. If two players oppose each other in this game, each has a team for which s/he rolls the dice to determine the outcome. As in any baseball game, the winning team is the one with the highest score, and therefore the winning Dice Baseball player is the one whose team has won the fantasy game.

The player whose team is at bat rolls two dice for each fantasy player who is at bat, then records the results on his or her box score. Each inning continues until there are three outs. Games are nine innings, and games go into extra innings in case of a tie, just like real baseball games. The roll of the dice determines the fate of the batter. The dice rolls are as follows:

1-1:	Single
1-2, 1-3:	Player has been put out
1-4:	Walk (base on balls)
1-5:	Strikeout
1-6:	Double play. If there are runners on base, the batter and the most advanced runner are out; no one advances. If there are no runners, the batter is still out
2-2:	Double
2-3:	Batter gets on, on an error
2-4:	Sacrifice fly; if no runners on, it's simply a fly out
2-5:	Strikeout
2-6:	Single
3-3:	Triple
3-4:	Player has been put out
3-5:	Strikeout
3-6:	Stolen base for the leading runner; batter

remains to take another pitch; if there are no runners, roll again

4-4:	Home run
4-5:	Strikeout
4-6:	Player has been put out
5-5:	Strikeout
5-6:	Player has been put out
6-6:	Single

Notes:

- Runners advance the same number of bases as the batter. Examples: If there's a runner on first and the batter hits a double, the runner automatically advances two bases and gets to third; if there's a runner on second and the batter hits a double, the runner automatically scores.

- Because each roll of the dice is an at-bat, rather than just a pitch, the game moves fairly rapidly.

- Though a casual player might keep the box score for a game, throw it away, and play again next time with a new lineup, a committed fantasy-baseball nut might play every night and keep exhaustive season-after-season records for each player, each pitcher, and each team. In fact, the committed Dice Baseball nut's mother (you?) might still be bugging him (or her) twenty-three years later to please get those darned old boxes of fantasy box scores out of the attic!

Got a couple of dice? Batter up!

SPELLING CHASE

Materials needed: Any commercial board game you already have around the house, such as Monopoly, Parcheesi, or Sorry, whose board has spaces for moving from a starting point to a finish; tokens from that game or any other, which will represent each player; either a deck of cards or one die; index cards or, alternatively, at least twenty card-sized pieces of paper; pen or pencil

This is a game for two or more children who are about the same age (but see "Alternative play" on page 14 for a variation that accommodates players of disparate ages), and one parent. The kids each try to be the first to get from Start to Finish, moving their tokens around the board by a combination of knowledge and chance.

The element of knowledge is in being able to spell a word correctly. The element of chance comes into play in the matter of how many spaces each player gets to advance after spelling a word right.

The number of spaces each player advances with a correct answer is determined by a roll of the die or, alternatively, if you don't have a die in any of the games you have, then by picking a card. If you are using cards, take all the aces, deuces, threes, fours, fives, and sixes out of the deck to use, putting the other cards aside, as you won't be needing them. Shuffle the twenty-four cards you have kept for use.

You, the parent, need to prepare for this game by writing at least twenty words within your children's ability to spell. Each word goes on one index card or piece of paper. Shuffle the cards or mix up the papers and place them upside down.

The players place their tokens on Start. Play proceeds from youngest to oldest. The youngest child rolls the die (or picks a card). The number that comes up is the number of spaces the first player will move his/her token if s/he correctly spells the word on the card (or paper) at the top of the pile.

The parent draws the top card and reads the word aloud. The child now has to attempt to spell it. If the child spells the word correctly, s/he advances the token the number of spaces on the board that correspond to the roll of the die (or draw of the playing card—the ace being equivalent to one). If the word is spelled incorrectly, there is no penalty, but the player does not get to advance any spaces on the board. Play now continues to the next-youngest player, and so on.

If all the word cards are used before the game ends, the parent shuffles them and uses them again. The game is over when one player reaches Finish. Unlike certain boxed board games, you do not need an exact number to cross Finish. That is, if the player rolls a five and only needs four to cross Finish, that's perfectly fine.

The fact that the youngest child rolls first gives him/her some edge over the older one(s) to compensate for the fact that the older one(s) may spell better. The other compensatory factor is the roll of the die or pick of playing cards. This element of chance makes it possible for a poor speller to win the game anyhow, if that player rolls more high numbers in spite of spelling fewer words correctly.

Alternative play: The parent may provide two (or more) decks of spelling words of differing difficulty for children of disparate ages, so that a seven-year-old and an eleven-year-old, for instance, can play this game together and compete against each other on even ground. The parent simply reads the top card on the deck of easier words for the seven-year-old's turn and the top card on the deck of more advanced words for the eleven-year-old's turn.

Variation #1: Reading Chase: This is a game for beginning readers. Instead of the parent drawing the top card, reading the word aloud, and requiring the child to spell it, the child draws the card, looks at the word, and is required to read it aloud, pronouncing it properly. If the children are currently learning the vowel sounds, the parent may wish to concentrate on such words on the cards as "HATE," "HAT," "MATE," "MAT," etc. If the children are just learning general vocabulary, any words suitable to the children's reading level will do.

Variation #2: Capitals Chase: The parent writes the names of the fifty states on the index cards, and each player, drawing a card, is required to name the capital of the state listed on that card.

Other variations: This game can be adapted to any age level and any subject. For kids learning simple addition, the index cards can have $3 + 2$, $4 + 5$, $9 + 9$ and so on. For kids learning multiplication, 9×3, and 4×8 and so on.

In fact, you can call the game Education Chase and, with different stacks of cards for different players of different ages, you can quiz your six-year-old on reading, your eight-year-old on division, and your eleven-year-old on the natural resources of foreign countries. For a parent willing to take the time to fill out lots of index cards, there's virtually no limit to the questions asked or the age range suitable. And of course, the cards are reusable, so the parent won't have to fill out new index cards every time the game is played, though adding new cards at frequent intervals is advisable as the kids get to know the answers to the existing questions pretty well, or because they advance to new grades in school and new levels of learning.

VERY SHORT STORIES

Materials needed: Paper and pens or pencils

This game is suitable for two, three, or six players. In it, you are making up a *very* short "story," precisely six lines long, about two people, according to a prescribed formula. The procedure varies slightly depending on the number of persons playing.

For three players: Player number one writes down the name of any female, real or fictitious, adult or child, that is recognizable to the other two players. It can be an older brother's homeroom teacher, a Smurf, Barbie (the doll), Mrs. Barnes next door, a friend of one of the kids, or even another player. The player should write small, right at the top of the page. Then that player folds the paper down so the name is not visible and passes the paper to the second player.

The second player, conscientiously keeping the paper folded and not peeking, writes the word "met" and then the name of any male, again real or fictitious, ranging from Bill Clinton to Larry Byrd to Mickey Mouse to Santa Claus. Again, the writing should be small to leave plenty of space, and again the paper gets folded down.

The third player, again conscientiously keeping the paper folded, and having no knowledge of the names that have been written down by the first two players, writes the word "in" or "at" or "on," followed by a place. This could be "in Goofy's house," "on the moon," "at the school book fair," "at a Michael Jackson concert," "in homeroom," "at the North Pole," "in the Sahara Desert," "on top of Old Smoky," "in the bathtub," or any other recognizable location, however ludicrous it may be. Again the paper is folded and passed.

Now it goes back to the first player, who wrote the name of the female in the story but has no knowledge of who the male is. This player writes, "He said," and follows it up with a short statement or question: "Would you go out with me?" "I hate spinach." "Clean your room!" "Is your mom strict?" "Supercalifragilisticexpialidocious." Then this player again folds the paper and passes it to the second player again.

This player, who wrote the name of the male in the story but has no knowledge of who the female is, has the job of supplying one line of dialogue for that female. The player writes "She said," and follows it up with, again, a short statement or question: "Let's play Nintendo," "I couldn't agree with you more," "Cowabunga," "You wouldn't kid me, would you?" "Bet you can't say that three times quickly!" The paper is then folded and passed one last time.

The third player now has it again. With no idea who the "hero" and "heroine" of the "story" are, the third player writes "So they" and follows it up with a brief action: "Did their homework." "Got married." "Went for a balloon ride." "Had sixteen kids." "Went on television together." "Invented dishes that clean themselves."

The paper is now returned to the first player, who unfolds it and reads the outrageous result aloud.

The round is over, and the players can proceed with another round. The player who was second should start first this time, and play should proceed around the circle in the same order, so that everyone has something different to write this time, and a different player gets to read the finished story aloud. (There are no points awarded for the player giggling the loudest!)

For two players: The game's the same, but you have to change the order of "He said" and "She said" to prevent the players who write the quotations from knowing who the speakers are. So the first player writes the female's name, the second player writes "met [male's name]," and the first player supplies the location. Then the paper is passed back to the second player, who writes "She said_____," leaving it to the first player to supply what "He said." The second player gets it back one last time to fill in "So they_____." Then the first player opens the paper and reads it.

For six players: It's also possible to play with six players, each one filling in one of the missing parts of the formula. In this case, it doesn't matter which comes first, "He said" or "She said," as long as it's agreed upon ahead of time.

THE GAME OF THE SEASONS

Materials needed: One die to roll to determine who will play first (optional), and one set of Seasons cards. To make the cards: Cardboard, tagboard, old file folders you can cut up, or similar; scissors for cutting; crayons or paints

Preparing the cards: You will need four cards for each player *plus four extras*. In other words, for two players you need twelve cards, for three players you need sixteen, for four players twenty, and so on. Cut all the cards of equal size; somewhere around the size of a standard playing card is fine.

Have the kids draw a tree on each of the cards. On each set of four cards, one tree should be bare and leafless, representing winter. One should have little dots of green, which are supposed to be buds, representing spring. One should be lushly green, representing summer. And one should have colorful leaves, some or all of the fall colors: orange, red, brown, and yellow, representing autumn.

Playing the game: Shuffle the cards and lay them facedown in a pile on the table. Each player rolls the die, and the player who rolls highest goes first. In case of a tie, those players roll again. If desired, or if you do not have a die in the house, another method of determining who will start can be used. Play will proceed clockwise from the starting player.

To begin, the starting player draws a card from the top of the deck and lays it down faceup in front of him/her. Each succeeding player does the same. When each player has one card faceup, play returns to the starting player, who draws the top card from the pile.

If the card drawn depicts the season following the season on the card that player already has in front of him/her, it goes faceup on the table. If it does not depict the next season in the cycle, the player places it faceup in a discard pile in the center of the table.

As an example, say that Sue, Lisa, Bob, Mom, and Dad are playing. If the first card Sue draws is a spring card, she now needs to draw a summer card. Lisa and Dad both drew an autumn card for their first cards, so they are both looking for a winter card next. Mom drew a summer card, and is now looking for a fall card, and Bob's first card was a winter card, so he needs a spring card next.

Play continues around the table, with each player drawing the top card from the pile and keeping it if it is the card needed next or placing it in the discard pile if it is not. Whether or not a player gets the desired card, only one card per turn may be drawn, and then it is the next player's turn.

When there are no cards left in the original pile, the discard pile is turned upside down, shuffled again, and returned to the table to be drawn from all over again.

Play continues until one player has drawn all four seasons in order. That person is declared the winner. If desired, play may continue to see who comes in second, third, etc.

BLANK JIGSAW PUZZLES

Materials needed: Cardboard, scissors, and pens or pencils

Half the clues in figuring out how to put jigsaw puzzles together come from looking at the interlocking pieces and seeing which piece looks like it fits together with which other piece; the other half come from looking at the picture itself and figuring out that if this is a hand it must go somewhere around here, or if this is a piece of the lake it must go somewhere around there.

How much more challenging it is to put together a puzzle with no picture on it! It's not pretty, and you won't want to gaze at the finished product, but putting it together is harder and therefore, in its own way, more fun.

If your children aren't too young, they can even make the puzzles themselves, and have still more fun by designing and cutting the pieces. If they're little ones, parental aid is called for.

With a pen or pencil, design the pieces of the puzzle on one side of the cardboard (or tagboard, or old file folders, or whatever you have handy). Feel free to erase and redesign. You or your kids can make the pieces as intricate and complex as your kids' frustration level will tolerate. The more pieces there are, the longer it will take to solve the puzzle—and keep the kids occupied.

If the cardboard isn't the type that's a different color on either side, you should lightly color one side of it, so the kids know which side goes up. You don't need paint or crayon, though you can do so if you wish. Pencil shadings will do fine, or you can mark a little X somewhere on each piece. Then the kids know to keep all the shaded or marked sides up—or down; it doesn't matter. Otherwise they could wind up trying to do something that won't ever work, because some of the pieces are flipped over.

When you're satisfied with the design, cut along the lines and present the challenge to the kids. If they've designed and cut the puzzle up themselves, and if you have more than one child, let them exchange puzzles, each trying to solve the other's puzzle. If you only have one child, or if they're of vastly disparate ages and one has designed a much easier puzzle than the others, they can still have fun solving their own puzzles.

If the puzzle proves too easy—or too hard—try again with another piece of cardboard. It's easy enough, it's fun, and the price is right.

DICTIONARY DEVILS

Materials needed: Index cards or card-size pieces of paper of a uniform size; pens or pencils; good dictionary (unabridged is preferable but not necessary)

This game for three or more players has been around a long time, and it's so much fun that now there's a boxed version. But you don't have to spend good money to have a good time. All you need is the materials listed above—and possibly a bandage for when you split your sides laughing.

This is not a game for little kids. Try this out with teens, literate preteens, and of course, very definitely, adults.

Each player gets a pen or pencil and a supply of index cards (or pieces of paper). One player is the moderator for the round; next round someone else gets a turn. Everyone needs to have an equal number of turns at being moderator, to keep the scoring fair. We'll get to that in a bit.

The moderator leafs through the dictionary to find a word unfamiliar to all the other players. (It's irrelevant whether the moderator knows the word or not.) After finding a suitable word, the moderator announces it, and if any player does know the word, that person speaks up. If no one knows it, play proceeds.

Each player now has to write down a definition that could logically apply to the word. The object is to invent one that sounds so plausible and so like a dictionary definition that it will deceive the other players into believing it's the genuine article. Each player also writes his/her name, or initials, on the card. While the other players are writing down their bogus definitions, the moderator writes the *real* one, from the dictionary, on a card just like the cards the other players are using.

All the definition cards are now turned in to the moderator, who shuffles them (including the legitimate definition) into any order, and then reads them aloud, slowly and clearly. The moderator should be careful to give no clue as to which definition is the real one.

After all the definitions have been read aloud (and repeated once, if anyone makes that request), every player in turn clockwise from the moderator has to vote for what s/he thinks is the *real* definition. The moderator keeps track of which definitions have been voted for. All players place their votes before the real definition is revealed. Players shouldn't giggle or say, "That one's mine!" until everyone has voted.

Now comes the scoring: A player who selected the actual dictionary definition gets a point. A player whose bogus definition is selected as the real one by another player also receives a point. The moderator gets no points, but as everyone will get an equal number of turns as moderator, it works out fairly.

The number of rounds you're going to play should be agreed upon in advance. If there are three players, and you have a whole evening in front of you, you might decide you're going to play nine rounds—that is, each of the three people will get to be moderator three times. If there are five players and everyone has to get up early tomorrow, you might only play five rounds, with everyone getting to be moderator once.

At the end of the agreed-upon number of rounds, add up the score, and the player with the most points wins the game.

One friend of mine recommends keeping a mop and bucket nearby in case a player wets his/her pants from laughing so hard. I've played this game *sans* accidents, but I can report a distinct shortness of breath from the giggles.

Dictionary Devils may belong in the category of "Quiet Games" because it's not active, but with the level of hilarity involved, *quiet* is definitely a misnomer!

ODD COUPLES

Materials needed: Paper and pens or pencils

This is a game that tickles the funnybone of kids of all ages, right up through the teens, and even parents can enjoy the odd match-ups that result during play. Any number from two up can play, and any child old enough to write can participate.

The premise is simple: To come up with funny, unplanned odd pairings of people, real and/or fictitious. Tear the paper into small bits, just large enough to write a name on. Distribute an even number of pieces of paper to each player. For just a pair of players, try distributing twelve pieces of paper per person per round the first time. For larger groups, give fewer pieces of paper to each player. The exact number is not important, as you will see in a minute; but it is only fair that each player gets the same number of pieces of paper, and it is most important that there is an even number of papers.

Each player now writes an equal number of names of males and females whose names are recognizable to the other players, one name on each piece of paper. The people may be real or fictitious, adult or child: A friend, a neighbor, a comic book character, a TV character, a movie actress, a President of the United States, the family's dentist—anyone whose name is recognizable to the other players. Each player must write the names of an equal number of males and females, however. Now fold each piece of paper twice (to avoid it coming unfolded), and place all the male names in one pile and all the female names in another pile.

Each player now takes a turn, going clockwise around the circle, picking one name from each pile and reading the two names aloud. Mr. Johnson, the math teacher, may be paired with Daisy Duck; older sister's boyfriend may get paired with Madonna; the babysitter may get paired with Willy Wonka; Abraham Lincoln may be paired with the (female) school bus driver. After names have been read, they are discarded. Continue until all the names are used up. Then pass out fresh paper and start again, with everyone trying to think up a fair number of fresh names, though some repeats will be inevitable.

Continue playing until the kids start getting tired of the game, which may take a while, or till all the same names keep coming up because no one can think of any new ones.

To get back to what I said earlier—and now that I've explained the game, you'll understand what I meant— the number of names each player puts in is flexible, as long as every player has an equal chance, putting in the same number of names as every other player. For a larger group, fewer names per person (say, four males and four females each) will likely result in fewer duplications of names. For a smaller group—say, two or three players—more names per person are needed to keep the game going longer. You don't want more than something like twenty-four total pairs, though, to keep each round from dragging on too long. By breaking to start another round, writing fresh names down, you're varying the activity and keeping the youngest family members from getting bored too easily.

This is not a competitive game; there is no scoring, no winner, just fun. And absolutely no skill is required beyond the ability to read and write. So, unlike many other games, it doesn't matter whether any given family member (or friend who joins in) is a sports whiz or uncoordinated, a math genius or the kind of kid who needs paper and pencil or a calculator to add 3 + 3.

The piles of names for this game *can* be saved and reused, but it's more creative to come up with new ones, and writing the names down provides a helpful change of pace in the game.

JOTTO

Materials needed: Paper and pens or pencils

This is a word game for two players. Both players divide their paper in half. On one side, each player writes a five-letter word that the other player has to guess. On the other side, each player writes the twenty-six letters of the alphabet.

After the players decide who will go first, the first player thinks of a five-letter word and says it, spelling it to be sure there is no confusion. The second player then tells the first player which of the letters in that word, if any, appear in his/her mystery word. Player #1 circles, in the alphabet s/he has written out, the letters identified as correct and crosses out the ones indicated as wrong. S/he should also write his/her guess down, in order to keep track as s/he goes along.

Let's say Player #2's mystery word is *ghost,* and Player #1 guesses *boats.* Player #2 would say, "*O, T,* and *S* are correct." Player #1 would circle *O, T,* and *S* and cross out *B* and *A.*

Now it is Player #2's turn to guess a five-letter word, and for Player #1 to say which of those letters appear in the mystery word. Play continues back and forth this way until one player guesses the other's mystery word.

Players are not allowed to ask specific-letter questions: "Is there a Y?" They must supply a word containing a Y and find out that way.

A player does not reveal in what position a correctly guessed letter is to be found. For instance, in the example given above, Player #2 told Player #1 that *O, T,* and *S* were correct letters but did not give away their positions. So it is possible for a player to know what the five letters are and still guess the word wrong.

As an example, let's say that *steam* is the mystery word. A player who has correctly ascertained the five letters may on his/her next turn guess *meats* as the mystery word and be wrong. The other player would say, "All five correct letters, but that's not my word." Play then reverts to the other player, who gets another chance to guess a word—perhaps getting the correct word—before the player who incorrectly guessed *meats* gets a chance to scramble the letters and come up with the correct word, *steam*.

The winner, of course, is the player who is the first to correctly guess the other player's mystery word.

WHO AM I?

Materials needed: One large box or bowl, one safety pin, and, for each player, one piece of paper or notecard and one pen or pencil

Each player thinks of a person—real or fictional, living or dead, live or cartoon—anybody. It could be Roseanne, Cinderella, Michael Jordan, Abraham Lincoln, Barney the Dinosaur, Huck Finn, or your next-door neighbor. Each player now writes the name of that person on a piece of paper or notecard, adds his or her name in the lower corner of the paper or card, and places the card in a box or bowl with everyone else's cards.

One player at a time is it. That person reaches into the box without looking and selects a card, handing it to any other player without seeing the name written on it. It turns his/her back to the player with the card, and that player pins the card to it's back. (If the person pinning the card on sees that the card bears, in the lower corner, the name of the player who is it and picked it—that is, if it is the card it himself/herself wrote—s/he puts it back in the bowl and it selects another card.)

It must now discover who s/he is by asking yes-or-no questions: Am I a fictional character? Am I a real person? Am I still alive? Am I female? Am I human? Do I work for the government? Am I an entertainer? Am I an adult? Do I have kids? Am I an American?

There is no limit to the kinds of questions that can be asked as long as they are answerable by yes or no. Kids will learn good critical thinking skills through the process of thinking up good questions to ask, as well as listening to the types of questions other players come up with when it's their turn to ask Who Am I?

You can play this for pure fun, not as a competition, or you can put a time limit on it, with everyone a winner who guesses their identity within the set time. If you do set a time limit, don't make it so short that no one will figure out their character, nor so long that people get bored waiting for their turns. Just how many actual minutes that translates to will depend on the ages of the players.

This is another of those great games that can truly be enjoyed by people of various ages together—little kids, teens, and parents alike.

FORTUNATELY . . .

Materials needed: Nothing but your imagination, and a library copy of the book *Fortunately* [Remy Charlip, Four Winds Press] if you don't own a copy

If you've read the children's book *Fortunately*, you'll know what this is all about; if not, check it out of the library. Anyhow, you'll get the idea as you read this.

The book can be a great springboard for some free-wheeling, imaginative fun. Everybody in the family gets a turn. Somebody starts off with a situation. Example: "I locked myself out of the house this morning." The next person chimes in with a Fortunately: "Fortunately, I had a spare key hidden under the doormat." The next person has to contribute an Unfortunately: "Unfortunately, a bird carried the key off as soon as I lifted up the doormat."

The next person has to supply a Fortunately: "Fortunately, the bird's nest was in a tree right in my backyard." The next person: "Unfortunately, I didn't have a ladder." Next person: "Fortunately, I was wearing spiked shoes and could climb the tree."

And so on, till no one can think of where to go from there and ends the story. Or till dinner's ready or it's time for bed. This is a great imagination-stretcher, and you'll be surprised at both the problems and the innovative solutions your kids (and you, yourselves) will come up with.

HAND-Y QUINTET

Materials needed: Washable fine-line markers, preferably in various colors; music on tape, CD, or record

This is a parent-child activity for little ones. Draw small simple faces on the pad of each of the child's fingertips, then turn on the music and let the finger-people dance, bow, and wave. One finger or thumb can separate from the rest for a solo.

If a very small child is afraid to allow you to write on his/her fingers, draw one face slowly on your own finger, saying, "Look, I'll draw one on myself. Here are the eyes, here's the nose, and here's the mouth. . . ."

You can probably alleviate any fear and get the child eager to begin.

This is a good way to make small children aware of various rhythms and get them used to keeping time to music by moving their fingers in time to what they hear.

OBSERVING FLYING JEWELS

Materials needed: Hummingbird feeder, sugar, water

This one does require an initial investment that's not as close to free as most of the other activities in this book, but a hummingbird feeder should only cost you around six dollars. Considering the length of time it will last and the enjoyment you and your kids will get out of it, the investment really seems minimal. The average family of four can spend more than that just taking the kids out for ice cream, if all four family members have a double-dip cone and a soft drink. After you've swallowed the last drop of ice cream and soda, what have you got left? Your six dollar hummingbird feeder, on the other hand, will give you years of delight observing these flying jewels.

There are about 20 species of hummingbirds in North America (and 400 more varieties in the rest of the Western Hemisphere), and these amazing, jet-propelled gems can be found in every state of the U.S.A. Your six dollar investment will provide the whole family with hundreds of hours of fascinating time watching, learning, and enjoying.

Hang the feeder where you can watch it through a window, but where a child can stand with his or her head only a foot away from where the birds will be drinking the nectar you'll provide them.

However, if there are cats around your house, please do not locate the hummingbird feeder any closer than six feet from the nearest rail, windowsill, the ground, or other surface from which a feline hunter can launch herself/himself. You don't want to be responsible for these beautiful birds being killed; you don't want to be responsible for their children being orphaned; and you don't want your child to possibly have to view the dark side of nature, if it happens s/he's watching when a cat kills a bird.

Hummingbirds very quickly become accustomed to the presence of people near their feeders, and a child can easily spend huge blocks of time watching the birds' comings and goings. With patience it is actually possible to induce hummingbirds to land on your fingers! You must be very patient, hold very still, and hold your hand right next to the feeding station. A friend of mine has had two different hummingbirds sitting on his hand at the same time, and regards that experience as one of the high points of a very eventful life.

It is not necessary to purchase commercially prepared food for your visitors. Mix plain white sugar into boiling water. (Proportions: One-third of a cup of sugar for every cup of water.) Many people color the water red, but that's not actually necessary. True, the birds are attracted to red, but most feeders are partly red, anyhow.

Besides, once the birds learn about the feeding station, they'll visit it regardless of what color the food is. In fact, you'll probably find that when you've taken down the feeder for refilling, the birds will come to the place where they're used to feeding and look around in puzzlement for the feeder they expect to find there.

Keep the feeder clean, and make new food every third day or so to keep the food free of molds or bacteria that might kill the birds. *Never use artificial sweeteners in lieu of sugar. The birds do not realize that the sweet taste contains no caloric energy, and they will starve*

to death. Also, never sweeten hummingbird food with
honey; that, too, will kill them.

A visit to the library (see "A Trip to the Library,"
page 103) can provide you with a book about birds in
general, including hummingbirds, or your library may
even have one on hummingbirds in particular. It will
give your child (and you) a wealth of information about
these birds who are capable of hovering and flying backward, and whose stunningly glorious colors are the result
not of pigment but of refracted light—their neck feathers
are actually prisms.

INTERNATIONAL HIGH FINANCE

Materials needed: Those coffee cans full of loose
change that you keep on the closet floor, and
some empty paper coin wrappers

Are you tired of accidentally kicking those cans full
of pennies, nickels, dimes, and quarters every time you
walk into the closet? Are you interested in showing your
young child how it pays to save? Are you interested
in helping your child improve his/her counting skills?
Enlist your child's help in bundling those coins up into
rolls the bank will trade for the long green stuff.

Get paper wrappers from the bank if you haven't
already got them sitting on a closet shelf, and dump
the money out in the middle of the dining room table.
(Doesn't it make a satisfying jingle?) Explain to your
child how many of each type of coin makes a roll, and
how much money one roll of each denomination of coin
is worth. Then show your child how to best count.

The safest way is to put the coins in stacks of ten
each. That way, if your child loses track at thirty-three,
s/he doesn't have to go back and start over from one.
Ten coins make a pile, and on to the next pile. If your
child loses track, s/he has only ten to count over at most.

And if s/he miscounts, the difference in height of one pile will be apparent.

The physical coordination required to insert the coins (ten at a time) into the tube, while blocking the other end with a finger, and then to jostle the change until it's all in an even stack again, is a good exercise in manual dexterity, too. If the child is old enough to count, yet too young for loading the wrappers, don't leave him or her facing mounting frustration; let your child do the part *you'd* find boring—which s/he won't find boring—and you do the part that involves manual dexterity.

If yours is a bank that requires your name and/or account number on the roll, let the child help you with that chore, too. Then take the child along with you to the bank, and let him/her see you get dollar bills (or ten-dollar bills, or fifties) in exchange for the coins. If you would normally just deposit the rolled-up coins to your checking or savings account, consider trading them in for greenbacks this time, just so the child can see that process. It's more meaningful for your child to see you getting the dollar bills in exchange for the coins, than to see you getting a piece of printed paper.

If you want, you can reward your child for her/his help with a crisp green dollar, or with a roll of pennies that s/he can trade in for two quarters. Or take one of those fresh greenbacks and treat your child to ice cream for services rendered.

FOOTBALL-CARD FOOTBALL

Materials needed: A few thousand of the bubble gum football cards that are probably spilling out of your child's closet and drawers and all over the dresser; paper and pen or pencil

This very simple playtime use of sports cards can keep a child quiet for hours—except for occasional outbursts of cheering when his or her favorite team upsets the defending Super Bowl champs! And Dad—and Mom, too!—can join in the fun if they wish.

The player may make elaborate schedules, pitting all the teams against all the other teams, use actual NFL schedules, or simply play various teams against various other teams without worrying about the big picture.

A game is played simply by choosing a single player's card at random from each of the competing teams, then comparing *all* the statistics—even height and weight— and scoring a point for the appropriate team each time that team's player bests the other one.

An example, as played by a forty-something player with a stack of 1958 NFL cards: The teams in question are the Detroit Lions versus the New York Giants. The players picked to represent the teams are Dorne Dibble and Frank Gifford. Gifford is 6′1″ Dibble is 6′2″. Score one for Dibble and therefore the Lions. Both men weigh (or did in 1958!) 195; no change in score. Gifford is 26 (on the card from 1958—even Kathie Lee is older than that now!) and Dibble is (in 1958) 28, so now it's 2–0 for the Lions. Both men have been pro football players for 6 years according to the card, so no change there. And Gifford's card serial number is 88, while Dibble's is 97, so it's a clean sweep for Detroit.

Got the idea?

The child's level of interest in football teams and players, and his or her pleasure in living in a fantasy world will determine how elaborate the record-keeping from such contests becomes.

Though I've presented this as football-card football, the same procedure can be applied to any sport for which there are sports cards; if your kids (or any other member of your family!) are hockey nuts, basketball fanatics, etc., they can play this game with the teams from their favorite sport the same way.

MULTI-COPY JIGSAWS

Materials needed: Cardboard; scissors; pens or
pencils; multiple copies of the same picture from
a magazine. Use an ad that appears in successive issues of the same magazine, or in two or
more different magazines you receive, or a picture
or ad that appears in both your copy and your
neighbors' discarded copy of a particular magazine

Have each child paste a copy of the picture in question on cardboard, then draw a jigsaw puzzle pattern
of cuts on the back of the cardboard. Parental help
may be needed with the scissors in cutting the pictures
up according to the kids' patterns, or if they're old
enough, they can do it themselves. Remind them that
the more intricate the cuts, and the more cuts there
are, the harder the puzzle will be to solve, but it will
be more fun.

Now mix all the pieces from the two or more copies
of the picture together, and you have a *real* puzzle to
deal with: pieces of multiple copies of the same picture
to sort out into two or more pictures.

You can also have the kids exchange puzzles after
they've cut them up, so that each child is putting together a puzzle whose picture is familiar but whose cuts are
unfamiliar.

SALVO

Materials needed: Paper and pens or pencils

Long before the boxed game Battleship or its electronic equivalent, kids were playing Salvo with pencil
and paper. Like the fancier, more recent versions, it's

a strategy game for two people—kids, adults, or one of each. This is a particularly good game for a child and adult to play together, as age and knowledge are not overbearingly advantageous, and kids are not as vastly outwitted as they are in some other games.

Preparing to play is easy:

On a piece of paper, each player draws two identical grids composed of eleven parallel horizontal lines and eleven parallel vertical lines. This will give the players two grids of ten squares across by ten boxes down. The rows going across are to be labeled *A* through *J*; the rows going down are to be labeled *1* through *10*. Now each square can be identified by a letter/number combination: *A-3*, *B-9*, *J-7*, etc. (If you have graph paper in the house, great! You can label ten of the rows across and down without having to draw the lines.)

Now each player draws a border around one set of two consecutive squares, two sets of three consecutive squares each, one set of four consecutive squares, and one set of five consecutive squares on *one* of the two grids s/he has drawn.

They can either be consecutive squares going down (such as *C-3*, *C-4*, and *C-5*) or consecutive squares going across (such as *G-7*, *H-7*, and *I-7*). They cannot connect diagonally. They cannot turn corners. They may touch but may not overlap.

These five sets of squares that have been marked are that player's ships. The other player is going to try to find those ships. By finding all the squares of each of the five ships, s/he sinks them. Here is how they are identified:

> A two-square-long ship is a destroyer.
> A three-square-long ship is a sub.
> A four-square-long ship is a battleship.
> A five-square-long ship is a carrier.

The players may each want to keep a list of the above identifications in front of them until they memorize them.

Player #1 starts by calling out a square—say, *C-3*. If *C-3* happens to fall within one of the sets of squares that Player #2 has bordered in as a ship, s/he calls out "Hit" and identifies which type of ship has been hit. If Player #2 says "Destroyer," Player #1 knows s/he only needs to find one other square touching *C-3* in order to sink that ship. If s/he says "Carrier," Player #1 knows s/he needs to find four other squares before the ship is sunk. If the square that was called out does not fall within any of Player #2's ships, that player calls out "Miss."

Whether it was a hit or a miss, it now is Player #2's turn to try to fire on Player #1's ships. Player #2 does the same thing, calling out a square by its letter/number combination. Player #1 must truthfully answer "Hit" or "Miss." Again, if it is a hit, s/he must specify which type of ship was hit, so Player #2 knows how many more consecutive squares s/he has to find.

When all the squares of a ship have been "fired on" by an opponent, the player whose ship it is must declare "Sunk."

You'll remember that each player has drawn two grids on his/her piece of paper, marking one grid with the positions of his/her own fleet. The other grid is for keeping track of his/her opponent's fleet. When a player calls out a square to his/her opponent, and gets a report "Hit" or "Miss," s/he should mark that square on his/her other grid.

A miss can be indicated with an *X*, with an *M* for *Miss*, or by whatever other means work for that player. A hit is best marked by writing down the letter of the type of ship hit: *D*, *S*, *B*, or *C*, so the player knows how many more consecutive squares s/he is looking for.

The first player to sink his/her opponent's entire fleet wins the game.

BANKRUPT YOUR NEIGHBOR

Materials needed: One deck of cards for two players; two decks of cards for more than two players. Incomplete decks are fine for this game

Bankrupt Your Neighbor is one of those card games, like War, that can last quite a long while, and the rules are simple, so young kids can play easily. Since you don't need a complete deck, this is a great way to utilize those decks that have one card or more missing or that have bent-cornered cards that are unusable.

Rules for a two-handed game: Shuffle the deck and divide it in half. If there are an odd number of cards, just put one aside out of play. It doesn't matter which one. And you don't literally have to deal in the traditional manner; counting out half the cards for one player and then giving the remainder to the other player will do fine.

Decide who will play first. Player #1 now turns up his/her top card and places it faceup on the playing surface. If it is other than a picture card or ace, Player #2 now turns up his/her top card and places it faceup on the pile the first player has started. Play continues in this manner until somebody turns up a picture card or ace.

The other player now has to "pay" the player who turned up the picture card or ace. S/he pays in cards, which are put faceup into the pile in the middle; the amount of payment is determined by the card that was turned up. If it was a jack that was turned up, the opposing player must pay one card; for a queen, s/he pays two cards, for a king, three cards, and for an ace, four cards.

If none of these cards s/he is paying with is a picture card or ace, all well and good. The player who was "paid" takes the entire pile of cards, both the payment and whatever may have been underneath it, and turns all those cards facedown, putting them on the bottom of his/her pile of cards.

If, however, the paying player turns up a picture card or ace in the course of payment, the debt is wiped out at that point and the other player now owes *this* player money for his or her picture card or ace, at the same rate of payment.

Play continues in the same manner, always paying at the same rate, always paying for a turned-up picture card or ace. Whenever someone successfully completes a payment without turning up a picture card or ace, s/he then turns one card up onto the pile in the center, and play resumes in the same manner it started, with each player playing one card at a time in turn into the center pile until someone turns up a picture card or ace, and the other player has to pay.

The game is over when one player has won all the cards, and s/he is declared the winner.

Rules for three or more players: From the first player, play proceeds clockwise around the table, and when one player turns up a card that requires payment, it is the next player in turn, clockwise, who must do the paying. If one player goes bankrupt, having no cards left, s/he drops out of the game and play continues with the remaining players, until only one is left, who is then declared the winner.

FELT-ART BOX

Materials needed: Empty cigar box or shoe box, felt or flannel scraps

Though this activity is particularly useful for long car trips, it also lends itself to any other time that a take-along project is called for to keep a young one from getting bored and restless, such as in the doctor's office waiting room or when accompanying Mommy on errands. You'll need one of these boxes for each small child you're keeping occupied.

You prepare it ahead of time by gluing a single piece of felt or flannel to cover the entire inside surface of the lid of a cigar box or shoebox. Try to avoid wrinkles. Also cut a generous number of pieces of cloth, preferably felt or flannel, into a variety of shapes and sizes. Various colors and patterns are great aids to creativity too. Include oblongs of different sizes up to four inches long, triangles, circles, squares, and random shapes and zigzags as well. Any and all small and medium-size pieces of fabric, including sewing scraps, will serve.

The lining of the box will serve as a miniature flannel board, and the child can assemble the pieces of fabric into an infinite number of figures, pictures, and scenes. The triangle that was a pyramid at the Columbus exit of the Interstate will be a mommy's skirt by Indianapolis and the top of a Christmas tree by Peoria.

When the artist-on-wheels gets bored and decides to pursue a different activity, the fabric pieces stow away neatly in the box for no-mess, no-fuss storage.

PARTLY CLOUDY WITH SUNNY FUN

Materials needed: A partly cloudy day

A good imagination and a day with puffy clouds of different shapes is all you need for this activity that takes kids off into the wild blue yonder in more ways than one.

Looking for pictures in the clouds is a great way to avoid boredom while driving, walking, or just passing time on a slow day. You'll find dragons, faces, giant birds, the proverbial castles in the sky, and who knows what other lofty constructions.

But take it one step further. After every family member finds at least one shape in the clouds (regardless of whether anyone else can see it), use all the different shape ideas to create a story. You can all chime in with different parts of the story as you think of them, make it a progressive story with each person taking a turn in a strict order, or ask, "Who can think of this story?" and let one family member make up the whole thing.

CREATIVE DAYDREAMING

Materials needed: Paper (preferably graph paper) and pencils

Have you ever thought about the kind of house you'd live in if money were no object? I'll bet you have—and I'll bet your kids have, too. One rainy Sunday when the kids are bored, pass out paper and pencils (with lots of eraser left on them) to everyone. Now let everyone design his or her own dream house. (*Everyone* means you, too!) The designs should include furniture as well as structure.

Anything goes—practicality is not a requirement here. We're talking daydreams. Would your kids like a glass roof so they can go to sleep looking at the stars and wake up viewing the sunrise? Would they like a brook running through the living room, so they can go fishing even in rainy or cold weather without leaving the house? (Dad, too, might like the idea of getting out of bed, going downstairs still in his pajamas, and catching a trout in the living room for breakfast!)

How about a kid's room with hooks, shelves, and pipe racks for clothes-hanging right in the room and not in a closet, because with no closet there's no place for monsters to hide? Or one wall covered with floor-to-eye-level built-in shelves for storing books, toys, and clothing?

How about a black velvet ceiling with glow-in-the-dark planets and stars painted on it? (I've actually seen that one!) How about a Pepsi machine in every room, or soundproofing covering the ceiling and all the walls of a kid's room, to allow music to be played loudly without bothering you "old folks"?

Some of their designs may surprise you and be extremely practical, and they may give you ideas you can actually use if you ever remodel the house or go house-hunting for a new one. Even if their structural designs are impractical, improbable, or unaffordable, their furnishing concepts may turn out to be partially feasible at some future time.

You may even learn something about your kids that you never knew before. Or one of them may learn that he or she has a great interest in, and possible future in, either interior decorating or architecture.

You may never win the lottery, and you may never live in your dream house, but there's no pricetag on daydreaming.

HANGMAN

Materials needed: Paper and pen or pencil

Hangman is a word game for two players. The players decide who will choose a secret word first; the other will try to guess it. After this round, they will reverse roles, with last round's guesser being the one to choose the secret word and vice versa.

Player #1 prepares by drawing a stick figure of a scaffold (a short line going across and an adjoining longer line coming down from it) and a noose (a circle at the far end of the horizontal line) on his/her sheet of paper. Art talent is not a prerequisite; a simple stick drawing is all that's needed.

Player #2 decides on a secret word, which Player #1 will try to guess. Player #2 writes the word down but conceals the word from Player #1 but does tell how many letters there are in the secret word. Player #1 draws that many dashes on his/her paper, each dash representing a letter to be guessed at.

Player #1 then starts by guessing any one letter of the alphabet. Player #2 must tell if that letter appears in the secret word; if it does, Player #2 must also tell Player #1 in which position(s) that letter appears. (It may occur more than once.) Player #1 writes that letter above the appropriate dash(es) on his/her piece of paper.

If the letter does not appear in Player #2's secret word, Player #1 must draw a line down from the hangman noose. This line represents a body. Player #1 now guesses another letter, and again either s/he is told that the letter is correct and where it appears, or that s/he must add to the figure of the person about to be hanged, this time drawing a stick-figure leg from the body.

On the third wrong guess, Player #1 draws another leg, on the fourth wrong guess an arm, on the fifth wrong guess another arm, and on the last wrong guess the head. Player #1 is now "dead," and Player #2 has won the game.

If, on the other hand, Player #1 succeeds in guessing all the letters before completing the stick figure of the hanged person, s/he wins.

Now Player #2 gets a turn at guessing a word that Player #1 selects. Play proceeds in exactly the same manner.

Should a player choose a longer or shorter word for the secret word? As with so many games, if you ask twenty people how they play the game, you are likely to get at least five variations. Some people play that there is no letter limit; some play that the word must be four letters, or that it must be five letters; some play that the word must be *no fewer than* four letters; some play that it must be *no more than* five, or six letters. Assuming you're playing that the number of letters is entirely optional, there is an advantage to a longer word and an advantage to a shorter word.

A shorter word is, on the surface of it, easier to guess, requiring fewer correct guesses. Therefore it would seem that it's advantageous to choose a longer word for your secret word. But a longer word, because it has more letters in it, is less likely to result in wrong guesses, enabling your opponent to get a better shot at guessing the right word before completing the drawing of the hanged person. Therefore, in some ways, it is actually advantageous to choose a *shorter* word for your secret word.

Like so much in this world, there is something to be said for both points of view.

BOXES

Materials needed: Paper, pens or pencils

This is a game for two or more players. On a piece of paper, draw 100 dots in a grid 10 dots across by 10 dots deep. Choose one player to go first. She or he makes a line from any one dot to any other adjoining dot, going across or up and down, but not diagonally.

The next player now makes a line anywhere on the grid according to the same rules: sideways or up and down, not diagonally. This line may adjoin the first line, but it doesn't have to. Each player in turn draws a line in the same manner.

The object of the game is to close in a box comprised of four lines, while preventing your opponent from doing the same. When a player successfully draws that fourth line that creates a box, s/he puts his/her initial in the box s/he has created and takes another turn. It is possible for one line to create two boxes simultaneously. The player drawing such a line initials both boxes.

This player's turn continues for as long as s/he can continue to enclose a box with one line. When s/he cannot enclose a box, and has to simply place a line that doesn't create a finished box, play reverts to the next player.

The game is over when all the dots have been connected and the grid is fully enclosed. The player who has created the most boxes (determined by counting the initials in the boxes) is the winner.

INVISIBLE INK SECRET MESSAGES

Materials needed: Lemon juice (one small lemon per child is more than ample for most messages), toothpicks or similar small pointed sticks such as twigs (one per child), small bowl for squeezing the juice into and dipping the toothpicks into

What kid doesn't love secrets and magic? Elements of both are combined when you write with invisible ink. The invisible ink in this case is lemon juice, squeezed into a bowl, into which is dipped the end of a toothpick (or small pointed twig).

The "ink" will be barely visible when the child dips the toothpick in and begins writing on paper, and it will disappear altogether when it dries. But when the friend who is the recipient of the secret message holds the paper up to a warm lightbulb, the message will magically reappear as faint brown letters. (The recipient should be given instructions in advance, or s/he's likely to think s/he's gotten a blank piece of paper in the mail and may just throw it away.)

You should only squeeze one lemon at a time, in case the kids write really short messages. Keep the other lemons handy, and if someone gets into a really lengthy epistle, you can always squeeze another lemon or two.

OLD MAID

Materials needed: Ordinary deck of cards (not a pinochle deck)

Most kids today grow up playing Old Maid with a special deck of cards manufactured for that purpose, but it isn't necessary. While the special Old Maid decks may have colorful pictures, all you really need to play the game is an ordinary deck of playing cards, which you probably have around the house (commonly known as a bridge deck—the same deck you'd use for Gin Rummy or Poker—in other words, not a pinochle deck). Remove the queen of clubs from the deck. The queen of spades is your Old Maid. Any two cards of the same number and color (e.g., two red fours, two black sevens, two red kings) make a pair.

For those of you who don't remember the rules from your own childhood, it's simple: After making sure the queen of clubs has been removed, the dealer deals out the entire deck to all the players. Players remove all pairs from their hands, placing them face up on the table so the other players can verify that they indeed are pairs.

Now the player to the left of the dealer begins the play by taking one card from any other player. If that card gives him/her a pair, he/she lays the pair down on the table. If not, the player retains the card in his/her hand. Players who draw the Old Maid from another player's hand should not give away that fact by groaning, giggling, or making faces, as it is advantageous not to let the other players know where the Old Maid is.

Play continues clockwise, with each player in turn drawing a card from any other player's hand. If a player pairs up all of his/her cards and has no cards left, he or she is a winner, and sits quietly by until the game is over. When the next-to-last player has paired up all of his/her cards, the remaining player will be left with the queen of spades—the Old Maid—and that player is the loser.

Old Maid can be played by as few as two players, or as many as can sit comfortably around your kitchen table or in a circle on the floor, though six players is a recommended maximum. For two or three players, it may be a good idea to use only half the deck. Otherwise the number of cards is unwieldy for small hands to hold, and too time-consuming for short attention spans to pair up in the initial phase of the game.

Recommendation: If you use only half the deck, use all red cards except for the queen of spades, which will make the Old Maid stand out even more sharply.

Note: If you and your friends got a little too enthusiastic at last week's Poker game, and the corner of one card got bent, or if you have a deck that only has fifty-one cards (where *did* that three of diamonds go?), Old Maid is a great game in which to make use of that deck. There is no need to have two red and two black of *every* number. There is no card that's essential except the queen of spades. If you're short a black seven, just remove the other black seven from the deck before playing. If you play without a pair of black sevens or red fours, it will not make any difference to the progress or outcome of the game.

ANTEATER

Materials needed: Ordinary deck of cards (not a pinochle deck)

Anteater is nothing more or less than the game of Old Maid in a politically correct version. For those who object to the term *old maid* and its literal implications, an animal everyone laughs at and nobody thinks is cute has been substituted as the card nobody wants to get stuck with.

The Anteater is, of course, an ace, specifically the ace of spades. Follow the directions for Old Maid (see previous item), but instead of removing the queen of clubs, making the queen of spades the Old Maid, remove the ace of clubs, making the ace of spades the Anteater.

Nobody wants to get stuck with an anteater—except, perhaps, someone in serious need of an exterminator!

BOOK-READING BASEBALL

Materials: Large piece of cardboard or posterboard, marker, colored pushpins, library cards for all participants

Though one child can participate in this alone, just trying to see how many runs s/he can score, competition evolves with two or more players, and the child has a greater incentive to read more books. You parents can participate, too.

On the posterboard or cardboard, each child (or a parent) draws a baseball diamond. Details don't matter; all that's needed is a home plate and three bases in a drawing that looks enough like a ball field to satisfy the child(ren). Alongside the diamond, or somewhere nearby, is a separate piece of paper for each player's box score. The point of this game is to reward the young reader for every book s/he reads. The reward is the thrill of making hits and scoring runs on the baseball diamond and in the box score.

Each time a child finishes reading a book other than a school assignment (and this little game is great for ensuring that reading is kept up over the summer), the child advances a pushpin along the bases on the diamond. When s/he reads the first book after starting the game, s/he sticks a pushpin onto first base. When s/he

reads a second book, s/he sticks another pushpin onto
first base while advancing the first pushpin onto second
base. The third book is a single like the first two were,
but the fourth book—and every fourth book thereafter—
is a grand slam home run. The bases are cleared, all the
runners come home, and the child has a score of 4.

(Most children, especially younger ones, find it frus-
trating to have read, for instance, six books, and yet to
be credited with only three runs, so it's a good idea to
clear the decks on a regular basis, and making every
fourth book a home run does the trick and gives that
extra, needed incentive.)

The title and author of each book is what's entered
in the box score. Many adults delight in the fact that
they've kept track for thirty or more years of every book
they've read; if the child begins the habit of such record-
ing at an early age, the satisfaction is even deeper.

Since success breeds success, the child who suddenly
finds a big red 4 on the scoreboard, after reading that
fourth book and scoring a homer, will probably work
extra hard to add pins to the bases again and work
toward turning that 4 into an even more impressive 8.

Variation: For the child who's into football and
couldn't care less about baseball, draw a gridiron rather
than a baseball diamond, and have the pushpins advance
ten yards for every book read, with a touchdown scored
every time a pushpin reaches the goal posts.

WORD GOLF

Materials needed: Paper and pen or pencil

Word golf is an endlessly varied game that can be
adapted to any level of difficulty, and it is suitable for
solo or group play. The game is simple: Two words of
an equal number of letters are provided; the player(s)
must change one word to the other, one letter at a time.

Each step must result in a valid word. The object is to make the transformation in as few steps ("strokes") as possible.

When the game is played solo, a player can give himself/herself two words, challenging herself/himself to see how few strokes s/he can complete the transformation in. When played in groups, one person can come up with the words and assign them to the other(s), then vice versa, or both/all players can agree on a pair of words and compete to see who can make the transformation in the fewest strokes.

How is it done? As an example of Word Golf, let's change *Star* to *Moon*. Remember, you can change only one letter at a time, and each change must result in a valid word:

> STAR to SEAR
> SEAR to BEAR
> BEAR to BEAN
> BEAN to MEAN
> MEAN to MOAN
> MOAN to MOON

Since each step is a stroke in Word Golf, you've changed STAR to MOON in six strokes. Not a bad score.

Now for another example, let's change *Slow* to *Fast:*

> SLOW to SLOT
> SLOT to SLAT
> SLAT to SEAT
> SEAT to FEAT
> FEAT to FEST
> FEST to FAST

Six strokes again—six strokes must be par around here!

One last example: Can a DOG become a CAT?

> DOG to DOT
> DOT to COT
> COT to CAT

Three strokes—is that cat good for a birdie?

Word Golf is a good game for families to play together. Since most play is with three- or four-letter words, kids of, say, nine or older can play on a nearly even level with older kids or even adults. Teens can compete quite evenly with adults. And anyone who plays gets their mental faculties sharpened.

CONCENTRATION

Materials needed: Deck of cards

Concentration was a game played with cards long before the TV version. You can play it with two players or more, either all kids or kids and parents mixed.

There are three ways to play. The simplest form is a good game for the really little set and is noncompetitive. The other two forms are competitive games.

In the simplest form, one player (let's say Dad) selects a certain number of pairs of cards from the deck. (For the purpose of this game, a pair is two cards of the same number and color, such as two red threes, two black queens, or two jokers.) The number of cards used will depend on the age of the child playing. For a little kid, all the red cards from two through seven may be sufficient. For older players, who are competing with one another, the entire deck may not be too great a challenge.

Dad shuffles the cards and puts them facedown on the playing surface. The child now picks two cards. S/he turns them over, looks at them, and if they're a pair, leaves them turned faceup and puts them aside. If they're not a match, the child puts them facedown and picks another card, keeping it faceup.

Let's say the first two cards were a red two and a red five. If the third card the child picks isn't a red two or a red five, s/he leaves it faceup and picks a fourth card. Assuming it's not a match to the third card, s/he turns them both back down.

But let's suppose that third card *is* a match to one of the first pair. It's a red two. Now s/he's got to remember where that first red two was. S/he turns over a card where s/he thinks the red two was. If that card was the red two, the child puts them aside, faceup. If not, s/he returns both cards facedown where they were and tries again.

It may take several tries, but eventually a matching card to an earlier card is going to turn up. Whenever it occurs, the player has to try to remember where to find its match. The player always turns up two, and only two, cards at a time, returning them to their facedown position if they're not a match. Play continues until all the cards have been paired and turned faceup.

In this version, best suited to the smallest set, there's no winner, just the satisfaction of having completed the task.

Variations:

Competitive version #1 for two or more players: Play is the same as above, except that a stopwatch or watch is used to keep track of how long it takes the player to pair all the cards. Then the second player takes his/her turn, also timed. If there are three or more players, each takes a turn. The winner is the one who pairs up all the cards in the shortest amount of time.

Competitive version #2 for two or more players: This is the most-often-played version. After the cards are shuffled and placed facedown, each player takes one turn at turning up two cards and hoping to pair them.

Let's say that Player #1 turns up a red two and a black five. Player #2 goes next and turns up a black two and a black seven. Player #3 turns up a red three and a red two. Player #1 now has to remember where both red twos were turned up and find them both. If s/he does, s/he gets to keep them. If s/he doesn't pair, Player #2 now has a chance to turn them up if s/he remembers where they were.

A player who turns up a pair gets another turn. When s/he fails to pair, play passes to the next player. The game is over when all the cards have been paired. The winner is the player with the most pairs.

GHOST

Materials needed: None, although you may want a dictionary handy to look up word challenges

Ghost is a spelling game for two players. The idea is to add on letters to an existing letter or string of letters without making a word. If a player spells a complete word or adds a letter that isn't contributory toward spelling a real word, that player gets a penalty: a letter toward spelling the word Ghost.

Example: Player #1 says *A*. If Player #2 says *N*, s/he has spelled *an*, a real word. This round is over, and s/he gets a *G*, the first letter of the word *Ghost*. But s/he isn't likely to make that mistake unless it's his/her first time playing, so let's say s/he says *B*. So far, so good. Now it's Player #1 's turn again. S/he thinks of the word *able,* which would end on Player #2's turn. A good choice. So s/he says L. Since *abl* isn't a complete word, the game keeps going, and it's Player #1 's turn again. If Player #1 can't think of another word beginning *Abl,* s/he is forced to say *E* and the round ends. Player #1 gets a G.

Perhaps, however, Player #1 thinks of *ablaze*. Instead of saying *E* and completing a word, s/he can say *A*. (*ablaze* would still end on Player #1 's turn and give her/him a *G*, but for the moment this maneuver stalls off getting a *G*; and there is always the chance that Player #2 will think of a different word beginning *abla* that *doesn't* end on Player #1 's turn.)

Sometimes a player doesn't know how to spell a word and erroneously calls out a letter that doesn't lead to a real word. Or a player may gamble that another player will think of a word, and so s/he calls out a letter that doesn't really lead anywhere s/he can think of. In either case, if the other player can't think of a real word beginning with those letters, that person can challenge. If the player who supplied the last letter cannot come up with a valid word, correctly spelled, s/he gets a *G*.

If a player already has a *G*, s/he gets an *H*. And so on, *O* and *S*, through the *T*, at which point that player has spelled *ghost* and has lost the game.

There are three ways to get a letter: By being forced into saying a letter that completes a word; by saying a letter that does not lead to a correctly spelled word; by being unable to think of a letter to add to an existing set of letters, when there actually is a letter that would complete or work toward completing a real word.

If Player #1 started the first round, Player #2 starts the second round, and it continues to alternate in this way, until one player has all five letters of the word *ghost*. That player, having gotten *ghost*, loses the game.

FAN TAN

Materials needed: Ordinary deck of cards (not a pinochle deck)

Fan Tan is played with a standard deck of cards (bridge deck). Deal all the cards out; if there is an

uneven number of cards dealt, and some players get
more than others, that's all right. As the deal passes
around the table from round to round, everyone will
have a turn at getting stuck with extra cards. The player
to the left of the dealer begins play, playing a seven if he
or she has one. If not, he or she says "Pass" and forfeits
that turn.

The next player clockwise then plays. That person
may play a seven or, if the first player has played a sev-
en, he/she may play the next higher or lower card in that
same suit. If he/she cannot make any of these moves,
this player must say "Pass" and forfeit that turn.

The next player has the same options. Additionally, if
the preceding player has played a six or an eight, this
player may now build down from the six or up from
the eight.

Play continues in this manner. When an ace is played
on top of a deuce, or a king is played on top of a queen
(in this game, aces are only low), that closes the stack
and ends play on it. The winner of the game is the
first player to get rid of all his/her cards. If desired,
you may continue playing to determine second place,
third place, etc.

Strategy: Let's say you hold the eight and king of
diamonds, but no low diamonds, and also a seven in
any other suit. When your turn comes, if the seven of
diamonds is exposed, it's advantageous to play your
eight of diamonds, rather than your seven of another
suit, to insure that the diamond stack is built up, rather
than down, to enable you to dispose of your King. That
other seven can always be played later.

✂ Miscellaneous Activities

OPEN MIKE NIGHT

Materials needed: None, unless you want to get elaborate about this and cut a fake microphone out of cardboard and put a chair in the center of the area that will be your "stage"

Kids are natural hams, and most kids love telling jokes. Put these factors together and you've got the makings of a family show. If your kids *can* sing, play a musical instrument—even a toy one—dance, or perform in some other manner, a full-fledged family talent show may well be in order. And if there's one who can't sing, dance, or play an instrument, he or she can tell riddles or jokes.

A parent can be the emcee, introducing each child in the family, who then gets "up on stage" (one area of the living room or family room, most likely) and performs or tells jokes and riddles. If the parent has a bit of ham in him or her, he or she can make a big deal out of it, saying something like, "Welcome, ladies and gentlemen, to the———[family name] club, home of great entertainment every Sunday night. Tonight we take pleasure in presenting some new young comedians for your listening pleasure. We know you'll give a great welcome to our young stars. Let's hear it for all of them now." (Pause for applause.) "Our first guest this evening comes direct from Ms. Anderson's first grade at Eisenhower Elementary. Let's give a big round of applause to————"

The kids get to feel like stars for a night. And even if their appearance on the family "stage" isn't the first step on the way to fame, it may be a small step toward boosting their self-confidence, their ability at and comfort with public speaking (a useful skill later in life), and their feeling of self-worth.

WRITE A FAMILY HISTORY

Materials needed: Paper, pens, possibly a typewriter or computer if you have one, possibly construction paper or cardboard and crayons or paints

Most families are scattered these days. Although grandparents may live longer, and at least one of the kids' great-grandparents may even still be alive, chances are the kids don't know them as well as you knew your grandparents, or as well as your parents knew theirs. Chances are good that your grandparents lived nearby. Chances are good that your kids' grandparents don't.

And that's a shame—for a lot of reasons. One of those reasons is that your kids are missing out on hearing family history. When did their ancestors first come over from the old country? What various countries did they come from? How old was Grandpa when he married Grandma? How old was Grandma when Daddy or Mommy was born? What were the great-grandparents' occupations? What other tidbits of knowledge, trivia, or interesting information are there that might be fascinating or important?

Now's the kids' chance to find out the answers to all these questions and more. There's probably lots *you* don't know about your own parents, grandparents, and great-grandparents, either! Start by getting the family together and coming up with a list of interview questions.

Let the kids pretend they're reporters, if they wish, about to interview interesting subjects for a book—which, in essence, is exactly what they'll be writing—a booklet. And by getting most of their questions down in advance, they'll avoid repeated phone calls—quite possibly long distance—to fill in missing facts.

Of course, some of the basic questions to ask each interview subject are: Where were you born? When were you born? Where was each of your parents born, and when? When were your parents married? When were you married? How long has your side of the family been in America, what relatives came over, and from where?

But the kids may also want to ask about favorite toys and games from the old days, schools attended and what they were like, occupations, pets, and other bits of day-to-day living that would interest them.

Parents can get in on the act, too. Aren't there questions *you'd* like answered?

Naturally, the kids (and you) won't want to limit yourselves to just the questions you've written down in advance. Like any good reporter, your kids are going to pick up on things Grandma or Grandpa says in response to their questions, and ask questions about that information. "So you lived on a farm? Where was it? Did you raise vegetables or animals or both? Did you ever see a cow have a calf? Did you help? Did you make your own butter? How is it done?"

Let the kids interview you for the book, too. Though getting a hold of you for interviews will be an easier matter, the kids can make a list of questions to ask both their parents in the same way they did with the older generation(s). And if you're a divorced parent, they may

need to make a list to ask the absent parent during a visit
or in the course of a phone call.

When all the information available has been compiled, the kids can write it down and turn it into a
book—or at least a booklet. If someone in the family—
preferably one of the kids—types, they can type it up
neatly. If not, the person with the most legible printing
can print it out longhand. The kids may want to put
the book in a binder from the store or just enclose it in
cardboard or construction paper covers, possibly decorated with paints or crayons. "The History of the——
—Family" is a simple, basic title; the kids (or you)
may be able to think of something more creative and
clever.

If you have a computer, why not print out a
copy for every member of the family? Each kid
can make whatever kind of cover s/he wants for
his or her own copy. Now each child will have
a copy to keep and share with his or her own
children in later years. Then *those* kids—your grand-
children—will know more about their great-grandparents
and even their great-great-grandparents than most kids
do.

A BIRTHDAY TAPE FOR GRANDMA
OR GRANDPA

Materials needed: Tape recorder, tape

Few grandparents live "over the river and through the
woods" anymore. Most of them, these days, are retired
in Arizona, Florida, or some other faraway place, or are
actively pursuing careers in New York, L.A., or some
equally remote location.

Relatively few kids today have the joy and comfort
of being able to walk over to Grandma's house for
fresh-baked cookies, hugs, and good advice, or even the

pleasure of Sunday drives to Grandma's. Few grandmas have the joy of seeing their grandkids that often, either.

And some kids clam up on the phone with Grandma and Grandpa, or cost-conscious Mama keeps the conversation short. ("It's long distance. Talk quickly.") If the kids are older, they're out playing or studying at the library or just hanging out with friends when their grandparents call.

But Grandma or Grandpa can still have the pleasure of hearing their grandkids' voices—and what would make a better birthday gift and card all rolled up in one? Lots of kids who get shy on the phone will blossom in front of the microphone of a cassette recorder. It's the natural ham coming to the forefront. And while not every family has a camcorder yet, virtually every family has some kind of audio tape recorder.

Suggest to the kids that the family make a birthday tape for Grandma or Grandpa, and give them each a chance to think about what they're going to say and/or sing.

You might want to start by saying, "Happy Birthday, Grandma," then having each family member identify himself/herself, parents and kids alike, "from Joannie"— "and Dan"—"and Beth"—"and Robbie." Then have the whole family sing a rousing chorus of "Happy Birthday to You."

After that, let each family member take a turn, starting with the youngest. Each person can say as much or as little as s/he wants, from giving birthday wishes to reporting his/her latest news ("I caught a frog yesterday, and I got a B+ on a spelling test, and the doctor gave me my tetanus shot and I hardly cried at all."), with as many details as they care to fill in. Little ones may want to sing a song especially for Grandma such as "Mary Had a Little Lamb," a "Sesame Street" favorite, or whatever songs they're most familiar with.

Families with a particularly creative member may want to write a special song for Grandma's birthday, perhaps written to the tune of a familiar existing song, or a family member might even write a little skit that can be acted out on tape by some or all of the family members. Even if the contents of the tape are just good wishes, news, and a chorus of "Happy Birthday" by the————Family Singers, it's a present Grandma or Grandpa or Great-Grandma or Great-Grandpa is sure to enjoy and to treasure over many years.

TELEPHONE

Materials Needed: None

When I was a kid, we used to play this one for pure fun, but my mother once told me of attending a charitable organization meeting where this game was played by adults as a means of showing how rumors spread, the story changing as it goes, and individual people or specific ethnic groups getting hurt in the process.

My point is that, while you probably want to just play this one for fun with your kids, you could make an object lesson out of it if you want, about not believing everything you hear.

To play Telephone, you need either a large family or a family with visiting friends or neighbors—you want at least five people for this game, and the more participants the better. Have everyone get in a circle, and pick one person to start. That person thinks of a sentence and whispers it fairly quickly and quietly enough that no one else hears, in the ear of the person next to him or her.

This person then whispers quietly and fairly quickly, in the ear of the next person, the sentence as he or she thinks s/he heard it. The message is passed from person to person until it gets back to the player who initiated it.

Inevitably, the message gets garbled along the way. When it gets back to the original player, s/he repeats it as s/he heard it, then states what it was that s/he originally said. The fun lies in hearing the difference between what the original message was and what it came out as by the time it got back to the source.

The message that the first player starts out with should make sense, but it doesn't necessarily have to be true. In other words, nonsense words such as supercalifragilistic-expialidocious are not what's called for here, but it can be a silly statement such as "Pink toads love purple frogs legs for Sunday dinner." It can be a statement of questionable historical truth (e.g., "George Washington wore false teeth made of wood"—I've read books disputing that supposed fact.) or a comment on the here-and-now (e.g., "I think Mrs. Johnson is the toughest teacher at Franklin.").

This is yet another of those delightfully noncompetitive games where there's no winner or loser, and where age is irrelevant since no skill is involved, and all ages can participate together on an equal footing.

SOAP BUBBLES

Materials needed: ½ cup of liquid detergent to ¾ gallon of water, preferably with 2 tablespoons of glycerine added

Kids all love blowing bubbles, and it's not necessary to buy the commercially prepared bubble kits for them to have this kind of fun. What's more, with three-quarters of a gallon of bubble mixture, there's plenty to go around for the entire family, so you can join in with the kids.

Combine the ingredients listed above and mix them well to get your soap bubble solution. A commercial wand isn't necessary, either. Your grandparents formed circles of their thumb and index finger to blow the bubbles through, and so can your kids and you. Just make a circle (an "OK" sign) by joining the tips of thumb and index finger, then dip into the bubble solution.

The two time-honored techniques are blowing into the center of the circle—hard enough to expel the bubble but softly enough that it doesn't break—and waving the hand through the air so the bubble is carried out of the circle.

Besides that method, an impromptu bubble wand of large or small size can be made out of items around the house. If you have thin wire that can be bent easily, bend it into several circles of varying sizes, leaving a handle below each loop. Now your kids have several bubble wands that will create different-size bubbles.

If you have an old pair of eyeglass frames that has lost its lenses, your child now has a double-bubble wand! Do you have an old pair of blunt-tipped rusty scissors that your child left out on the porch, where they got wet? They may not be great for cutting paper anymore, but the handholds make good bubble wands if the child is old enough to hold the blade end as a handle respectfully.

Paper clips or twist-ties can be bent into small circles and pressed into service as bubble wands. Look around your house for anything circular and open, or anything that can be easily bent into a circle shape with a handle attached, and that won't be hurt by dunking it in water.

Besides simply blowing bubbles for the sheer joy of it, kids and parents can have bubble contests (who can blow the biggest), bubble races (who can blow a

bubble and then puff on it to get it the farthest before
it breaks), and bubble fights (each bursting the other's
bubbles).

SPELLING/MATH BEE

Materials needed: None

Among the fun activities that also serve an educational purpose are old-fashioned spelling bees and their
counterpart, math bees. In fact, there are few subjects
that can't be the topics of bees. The only limitation here
is that this isn't a game for an only child (unless there
are visiting relatives, neighbors, or friends to include in
the fun), and it's not as much fun for a two-child family
as it is for three or more. This is one case where the old
saying, "The more the merrier," definitely applies.

The premise of a spelling bee is straightforward: Each
contestant in turn is given a word to spell. If the child
spells it right, s/he stays in the contest. If s/he spells it
wrong, s/he's out of the game. The last one left is the
winner.

Of course, instead of spelling, the question could
be "What's 3 × 9?" or "What's the chief product of
Sweden?" or "In what year did the Civil War end?" or
"Name the capital of Switzerland" or "Define *egregious*,"
depending on the topic of the bee.

The parents should ask each child a question suitable
to his/her age and grade level; in this way the game isn't
weighted in favor of the older kids.

To keep the game from being over too quickly, a
number of rules can be devised to liven things up. Two
such are:

- A player isn't counted out of the game until s/he's
  gotten three wrong answers.

or

- A player is counted out after one wrong answer, but one round does not constitute the whole bee; the winner for the evening is the one who has won the most rounds at the end of the evening (a certain time limit having been set ahead of time).

Feel free to invent other rules that will make things livelier or more interesting for your own particular family.

FLY A BUTTERFLY

Materials needed: Bright paper, a very small cork, and a large spool (wood is preferable, but plastic will do)

Fold a four-inch-square piece of bright paper in half and draw one-half of a butterfly on it, making the fold of the paper his stomach. Leaving the paper folded, cut out your half-butterfly. When you unfold the paper, you'll have a butterfly with two wings the same size.

Paste your butterfly's stomach to the large end of the cork, putting the cork at just about the center of the stomach. Place the smaller, tapered end of the cork in the hole of the spool. Now put your mouth over the hole at the other end of the spool, point the spool upward, and blow sharply through the spool. The butterfly will shoot up and then drift slowly down.

BOOK CHAIN

Materials needed: Construction paper in various colors, scissors, pen, tape, books (owned or borrowed)

This activity encourages the whole family to read books.

Cut strips of construction paper about one inch wide and eight or ten inches long. (Whatever length you settle on, all strips should be identical.) Put them into a basket for use by all family members.

Each time a family member finishes reading a book (other than a schoolbook), s/he writes the name of the book and its author on a strip of construction paper, forms the strip into a circle, and tapes it closed. Each successive book title and author goes onto another strip of construction paper, each of which is looped through the ring before it and taped into a circle to form a link in a chain. The more books each person reads, the longer his or her chain will be.

You can tape the first link of everyone's chain to the ceiling or the top of a door and race to see who is the first to have his or her chain reach the floor, or each family member can keep his/her own chain, with everyone measuring their chains against each other periodically to see whose chain is the longest. The more books you read, the longer your chain will get.

It is not appropriate for a fourth-grader (assuming s/he reads at fourth-grade level) to read a bunch of first-grade-level books in order to be able to quickly add many links to his/her chain and come out ahead.

HOBO LUNCH

Materials needed: Lunch including special treats for the kids, one bandanna or one square of fabric about two feet square for each child, one stick for each child

Some families go on picnics so seldom that any picnic is a big deal and needs no added attractions to make it a special treat. Other families picnic frequently, particularly if they live near a park or have a large yard with a picnic table, and kids in these families can get to feeling very ho-hum about picnics all too quickly.

Well, here's a way to spice up picnics for kids like these. Instead of packing a picnic lunch in the cooler for everyone in the family, or packing each kid's lunch in his or her boring old school lunchbox, wrap the kids' lunches up hobo-style (being sure to include at least one special treat or goody).

Place the lunch in the middle of a bandanna or square of fabric, tie the corners securely together, and knot the whole thing on the end of a stick. A small branch is preferable, though a sturdy stick from an old balloon or other toy may be used.

Now let each child carry his/her lunch over the shoulder, hobo-style. It's just a little touch, but it adds a whole new flavor to the picnic fun for the kids and disperses the blahs.

FINE FEATHERED FRIENDS

Materials needed: **None except possibly a library book on birds and binoculars, if you already have them**

Bird-watching is interesting for all ages, and can be as simple as keeping an eye out the window for the various varieties of birds in your area, with attention to the fact that different species may be around at different times of the year. Early morning and evening are often the best times to spot them.

Let the kids pay attention to such details as the different songs the different species sing. The kids may get proficient at knowing what bird they're hearing, even before they see it. They may take an interest in what and where the different species eat, as well.

If you aren't able to identify all the various species of birds that the kids spot, a trip to the library to borrow a book identifying birds may be in order (see "A Trip

to the Library," page 103). The kids may want to keep
a list of birds they spot, including the dates. A seasonal
pattern may emerge.

If the kids really get into bird-watching, you can go
on field trips, bringing a pair of binoculars if you have
one, though it isn't essential. Another activity is to build
(or buy) a birdhouse and/or bird feeder. You can build
them with items such as scrap lumber, egg cartons, and
plastic milk bottles, for little or no cost.

The kids may want to try drawing the birds they've
seen. If they're keeping a log of birds they've spotted,
the drawings can illustrate it, but even if they aren't
logging what they spot, the drawings can be fun.

FRIENDSHIP BOATS

Materials needed: Wood; small jar with a tight-
fitting lid; small evergreen branches and/or dan-
delions and clover; saw and/or nails; paper and
pen or pencil; proximity to river or lake. Optional:
Short, fat candles and matches; glue

This one's for older kids who can write fairly well
and can use a saw and nails responsibly, or younger
kids can enlist a parent's help with the construction end
of it. The premise is that you start by constructing a
boat and end up—hopefully—by constructing a new
friendship.

You don't need to buy lumber for the boat if you or
a friendly neighbor have a workshop in your home. You
can saw a too-large scrap piece down to size or use scrap
bits and nail them together if you don't have one piece
large enough. Saw and/or nail the wood to the size of a
small-raft. The actual size is your option, but why not
try about a foot and a half long.

Decorate the raft with small branches and/or flowers.
(If you're a boy, and that doesn't appeal to you, skip

the branches and flowers rather than skipping the whole activity.)

Write a note including your name and address. Tell something about yourself—maybe your age and school grade, your interests, your favorite activities, or anything else you'd like someone to know about you. Use either a pencil or a waterproof pen or marker. In case water gets onto your note, you don't want the ink to run.

Now put your note in the jar and close the lid tightly, perhaps taping over the lid if you wish to make the seal even more watertight. Put the jar on the boat, possibly gluing it down to lessen the chances of its falling off the boat into the water.

It's more spectacular to sail the boat at night with candles on it. If this is parentally sanctioned, and assuming there's no drought, dry riverbank foliage, local laws prohibiting it, or other reason why the candles are unsafe or unwise, attach several short, fat candles to the boat using melted wax to hold them in place. Now to go the river or large lake after sundown, light the candles, and push the boat away from the shore. Enjoy the glow of the boat as it floats out of your life and into someone else's.

Now wait and hope that your note got into the hands of another child, one interested in carrying on a correspondence with you. You might have to launch several such boats before a note gets into the hands of an interested correspondent. Boats can capsize, land in the hands of adults or of kids who are the wrong age to correspond with you or feel they have nothing in common, but you might luck out and make a new pen pal or friend this way. I know of one girl who has carried on a three-year correspondence with a pen pal she met through a friendship boat.

GAZE AT THE STARS—
AND NOT MADONNA!

Materials needed: Telescope, if you already have one; library book on astronomy for kids

While I'm not recommending that you spend big bucks for a telescope, some households already have one, and if your kids are fortunate enough to be part of one of those households, it's never too early to get them interested in the other kind of stars.

If you don't have a telescope, they can still see the stars with the naked eye. Point out the various stars and constellations to them. They may be familiar with some names of heavenly bodies, either from school or from some knowledge of astrology. Now's a good time to point out the differences between astrology and astronomy, as well as how the questionable field of astrology derives from the existence of unquestionable stars and constellations.

A look at the stars can be a great springboard to learning a few facts such as that our sun is actually a star, and that the evening star and morning star are actually planets.

Did your kids know that the north star they see at night (assuming you haven't bought this book in someplace like New Zealand) isn't visible to residents of Australia and other southern hemisphere locations? In fact, that discussion could lead in turn to one about the seasons being different in the southern hemisphere, and how Christmas in South America and other southern hemisphere locations is warm and festivities may involve swimming.

And that discussion, in turn, can lead to one on how holidays are celebrated differently in different countries and how, in fact, some countries have different holidays from other countries altogether. (Do your kids know that

Saint Nicholas comes to kids in some Old World countries on December 5th, which is Saint Nicholas Eve?)

If you don't know all the answers yourself, that can in turn lead to a trip to the library (see page 103) to borrow books that will fill in the blanks.

To think it all started with a little stargazing. (And your kids thought the stars were just for "Star light, star bright" wishes!)

WHAT'S COOKIN'?

Cooking is a great way to spend time with your kids. If you're a busy parent—perhaps if you're a family of two working parents, or a one-parent family, or even if neither of the above is true—on a day when you have little time for the kids yet want to be with them, involve them in the kitchen with you. (Fathers, we're talking to you, too!) Dinner has to be cooked, regardless of how busy you are. Here's a great chance to accomplish something necessary and spend time with the kids and teach them a valuable skill, all at the same time.

How much you can involve the kids in your cooking will depend on how old the kids are and what you're preparing for dinner. Obviously, there's more opportunity for involvement in a simple dinner of meatballs, spaghetti, and sauce, or broiled chicken, corn, and salad, than if you're making beef Wellington; but in virtually every meal there's someplace where all but the youngest ones can help.

If you're not knee-deep in a recipe that requires intense concentration, you and the kids may find that the time you spend together in the kitchen is also a good time for conversation. This may be when the kids talk heart-to-heart, confide problems, ask serious questions, or just tell you how much they love you.

You can even set aside one night a week when it's the kids' night to cook, complete with planning the menu and maybe even helping shop for the food. (They'll have to learn sometime how to spot a good cut of beef, fresh-looking fish, ripe vegetables, or just a good bargain.) You're there to help, guide, and advise, but it's their night to star in the kitchen.

Whether they're helping you or doing it themselves (with help from you), make the occasion both fun and a learning experience, as well as a time for togetherness.

Younger kids can learn about the different food groups and generally healthy foods; older kids can learn about fat and protein content, counting calories, watching out for cholesterol, and any particular dietary needs of individual family members.

Tips
- Kids love garnishing foods: sprinkling herbs, decorating with cut-up parsley, making carrot curls, orange twists, or radish rosettes, or coming up with innovative garnishes of their own. They also often like to arrange cold cuts and cheese in a pretty pattern.
- Kids love secrets, so let them in on any secret ingredients you may have that make your stews, soups, or other recipes special. Emphasize the word *secret* to them.
- Ask them to set a pretty table. They may groan at just being asked to set the table, but occasionally tell them you want the table to look special (this won't work if you try it every night) and ask them to be creative. They may use a vase of flowers from the living room as a centerpiece or decorate with a crayoned paper plate, but let them be inventive. For a holiday table, they can make construction-paper place mats crayoned with the holiday theme, or any other reasonable (or semi-reasonable) decoration they think of. Don't pooh-pooh an off-the-wall idea if there's no practical reason why it needs to be discouraged. (For example, you'd need to discourage using a doll with

flammable hair as a centerpiece between lit candles, and Tommy's ant farm isn't what you want to stare at during dinner either, but if their outrageous idea isn't unsafe or repulsive, let them try it out.) Remember, you're trying to encourage participation, creativity, and self-expression.

FAMILY BAND

Materials needed: Glasses full of various levels of water, bells, hardcover book or other surface that will make a thumping noise when hit, anything else you have in the house that can make a musical (or percussion) sound

Your kids don't have to be musical geniuses to form a family band. They don't even have to own instruments!

With a little experimenting, eight different glasses can be filled with varying levels of water to achieve the eight notes of the scale when struck with a fork, spoon, or knife. Another child can thump on a book, the bottom of a pot, a large plastic food storage container, or anything else that will make a satisfyingly drumlike sound. And another child, if you have three, can ring a bell (jingle bells from your Christmas ornament or decoration collection) in time with the music.

If you have more than three kids, or you parents want to join in with more than just singing, additional percussion instruments can be found around the house—for example, two empty cardboard rolls from paper towels or toilet paper make a great sound when clapped together—but in the case of noisier instruments, play quietly, or you'll drown out the water glasses and bells.

Simple songs to figure out that use only those eight notes include, appropriately, "Do-Re-Mi" ("Doe a deer") and, just as appropriately, "Jingle Bells."

HOW LONG IS A MINUTE?

Materials needed: Clock (or watch)

How long is a minute? According to an old "Dennis the Menace" cartoon, that depends on whether it's a real minute or a "wait a minute."

Little kids often have trouble understanding concepts of time. (This is not at all the same thing as learning to tell time, a different skill, even though the two are related.) They don't have a good grasp of what a minute is. Here's a way to make it clearer to them.

Having kids see how many times they can do something in one minute is a great way to help them learn about time. Combine it with showing them a minute on a clock or watch, preferably an analog timepiece rather than a digital one.

If you have a timepiece with a second hand, start by sitting them in front of the clock and having them watch the second hand sweep around. Show them that when it gets "from here around and back again," it's a minute. If you don't have a timepiece with a second hand, show them with the minute hand. "When it moves from here to here. . . ."

Now let them see how much they can do within that time. While you're timing them, let them see how many times they can walk around the living room, or run around the yard. Let them build a wall of blocks while you time a minute, or go as far as they can in making their beds, or whatever other time-takers you can think of; stop them when the minute is up.

If you can think of fifteen one-minute time-takers, point out at the end of them that fifteen minutes has elapsed, explaining it and showing it on the clock. Now they have a clearer comprehension of the concept "In fifteen minutes."

Before long, your kids will have a better grasp of time concepts. When you say, "We can leave for the store in ten minutes," they won't be asking, "Is it time yet?" thirty seconds later and every thirty seconds thereafter. They may even have a good grip on estimating how long it should take to accomplish specific tasks.

COUPON MATCH

Materials needed: Coupons you were planning to bring to the supermarket

So what if this isn't really a game? The fidgety little ones accompanying you on a shopping trip to the supermarket won't know that, and it may slow them down a bit from the endless round of "Buy this? Buy this!" and "When can we leave?"

This works fine with just one child and is even better as a competitive game for two or more. Give or show the children a few of the coupons you're planning to use for items you're shopping for today, and tell them to keep their eyes peeled for those products. Let them hold them to refer to them if they wish.

If you've only got one child with you, present it as a challenge: "See if you're eagle-eyed enough to spot these things on the shelves." With more than one child, it's a competition: "See who can spot each of these things first."

Of course you can choose to give a prize—perhaps a healthful snack like a small box of raisins—to the winner, but there really needn't be a prize. Kids like to compete for the sheer joy of being a winner, and they shouldn't learn to expect more of a prize than simple satisfaction *every* time they succeed at, or do best at, some task or competition.

MODEL T FOR VERY YOUNG "DRIVERS"

Materials needed: Three or four big cardboard boxes; wallpaper paste; old pie pan with a hole in the middle; two tin cans, washed out, with the labels removed; knife or scissors to cut cardboard with; around five brown paper grocery bags; masking tape; nut and bolt that fit the hole in the pie pan; paint, preferably glossy enamel in a bright color; three-inch paintbrush

This is a project that you, the parent, will construct, and your three-to-five-year-old will play with.

Place the boxes in various configurations until you can visualize a rudimentary car out of them. Specific placement instructions are pointless as it will depend on the number and size of cartons you have acquired, and their size in relation to each other. Generally, you want two lower boxes, one each for the front and rear of the car, and a taller box for the middle, unless you have to substitute two smaller boxes for a larger one somewhere.

Use masking tape to hold the boxes in position. Now cut out windows. Make the side windows dip deeply enough that the child can get in and out of the car through the windows. You are not going to try to cut working doors out of the cardboard. If you choose to cut out a back window, make it small, so most of the back of the carton remains as support for the roof of the car.

Mix at least a quart of wallpaper paste. Brush the paste onto the seams where the boxes join. Cut strips from the brown paper bags, each at least two inches wide, and apply glue to one side. Place strips of brown paper over the seams to hold the boxes together at the seams. Also use paper to reinforce the cardboard at any points where there will be stress. Allow the paste to dry thoroughly.

The pie pan is the steering wheel. Use a box flap as

the dashboard and affix the pan to it with the nut and bolt. Leave the nut loose enough that the steering wheel can be turned easily.

Use masking tape to assure that the edges of the tin cans, which will be the headlights, are not sharp. Decide on the spots where you want to place the headlights; trace a circle around a can at each of these points. Now cut the holes slightly smaller than the circles you've drawn, so the cans will fit in snugly and stay in place. The headlights can be further steadied and strengthened by being taped on the inside, as well.

It will take two coats of paint to cover the car properly. Allow the paint to dry between coats.

You can make a license plate out of cardboard (or whatever you have handy), customizing it with the child's name and age: JUSTIN-4, for instance.

You can customize your car with other things, such as contact paper, trim you can buy at a fabric store, spools for knobs on the dash, drawer knobs or handles on the outside doors, even plastic wrap for glass on the back window.

Happy motoring!

CONSULT YOUR LOCAL COLLEGE

Materials needed: None

With more and more families getting their news electronically, the number of families who don't read the newspaper is increasing. If you're one of those families, you may not have seen notices for the many performances, courses, and other activities your local college probably offers, some of which would be of interest to your whole family, kids included.

Some colleges offer programs in the arts for young children, teaching rhythm band or more advanced instruments, art in various media, even puppetry. Most colleges with drama or music departments offer performances by their students—frequently free of admission charge—some of which are aimed at children or are suitable for children. Drama departments, for instance, often give performances of kids' shows or of well-known musicals.

Many colleges present professional touring companies performing dance, music, drama, or other performances such as mime for a very nominal fee. If your local college is sponsoring an art show, maybe now is the time to introduce your kids to sculpture, paintings, or whatever is at hand.

Call your local college(s) and ask what programs they have planned that are suitable for families with kids the ages of yours.

TIN-CAN TELEPHONE

Materials needed: Two empty cans with the tops removed, and washed out, which a parent has inspected to make sure there are no sharp edges; a long length of string (perhaps six feet); hammer and nail for piercing the cans

Long before the age of electronic toys, and long before cordless telephones existed at all, kids loved to play with tin-can telephones. Even now that there are relatively inexpensive toy walkie-talkies, you still can't beat the price of a tin-can telephone, and it's still fun for the young set. It's also not likely to be damaged by being left out in the rain, it's impervious to being dropped, and should some calamity befall it anyhow, like the dog chewing the string, no money's lost and it's easy and cheap to make a new set.

A parent should do the piercing of the cans, driving a nail through the middle of the bottom of each of the pair of cans, then inserting one end of the string through each

can. Knot the string on the inside, and *voila!* You've got
a set of tin-can telephones.

In case you don't remember your childhood, or in
case you led a deprived childhood that was tin-can-
telephoneless, one kid talks into one can while the other
kid puts the other can to his/her ear and listens. The
voice travels along the string. Then they reverse positions, and the second one listens while the first one talks.
Simple? Fun! Free!

REAP WHAT YOU SOW

Materials needed: Seeds, empty egg cartons

Raising your own plants, herbs, and vegetables can
be fun, and in the case of the vegetables, a real money-
saver as well. You don't have to live in the country or
rural suburbs. Even urban dwellers can raise plants or
herbs in a window box—and possibly something like
tomatoes, as well. A patio offers even more options.
Here's a project the kids can dig into literally as well
as figuratively.

Start the seeds in egg cartons. Give them plenty of
light, and when they have two or three leaves, transplant
them to a larger pot. Be sure to follow any differing directions on the individual seed packets. Fertilize
your plants, herbs, or veggies, and don't forget to water
them—all chores your kids can at least participate in if
not take over entirely, depending on their ages.

Marigolds and nasturtiums are good choices among
flowers, because they grow quickly and bloom all summer long. Tomatoes are a good veggie to grow; it's fun
to watch them ripen, and you can grow them in pots.
Chives, garlic, and mint are good herbs for small spaces,
but don't rule out other herbs, flowers, or vegetables if
you have more space.

If you have a decent-size garden to play around in,

let each child have his or her own patch in which to grow whatever catches his or her fancy—with a little guidance from you to be sure it's something that will grow in the climate where you live. Even if you're an apartment dweller, *sans* patio, why not give each child his/her own window box?

Your kids may even be tempted to eat veggies that they'd normally reject, if they're home-grown, do-it-yourself projects that the kids can take personal pride in. "I grew it myself" is a powerful temptation to sample the goodies.

CLIP COUPONS

Materials needed: Scissors, newspaper and/or magazines

It's never too early to involve children in the concept of saving money. Clipping coupons also involves them in shopping and menu planning. And setting up an informal filing system for the coupons fosters good organizational skills. They can arrange the coupons according to product: Cleaning supplies, personal care products, cereals, beverages, etc.

They can even learn a little bit of economics by comparing coupons of rival brands and figuring out which of two products—say, cereals—they like offers the most attractive coupon. (Which cereal offers more money off? Which cereal will wind up being cheaper after the cents-off are deducted? The answer may not be the same both times.)

Have the kids search newspapers and/or magazines for recognizably familiar brands of items you use. Many coupons feature photos of the products, so even very young children can recognize familiar products. (They can also look for items they'd like to try—a new brand of cereal, perhaps.) Then have them cut out the coupons and organize them, either in a little metal file box or with paper clips.

For a related activity, see "Coupon Match," page 74.

COMPILE A FAMILY RECIPE BOOK

Materials needed: Collection of family recipes, typing paper, heavy cardboard 6 × 9″, pieces of fabric or wallpaper 6 × 9″, heavyweight construction paper 5 ¾″ × 8 ¾″, rubber cement, cloth tape

This is a two-part project: First you have to collect the recipes; then you make the book. The recipes will ideally range from simple foods that at least the mid-range-age kids can prepare now to complicated family heirloom recipes that they'll only be adventurous enough to try when they reach maturity but will be glad they compiled while they had a chance. As the kids strike out on their own, they'll be glad to have the family recipe book to refer to.

The ideal compilation will include at least one recipe from every family member, so it will serve as a remembrance in time to come, as well as a recipe book. Every family member includes grandmas, aunts, cousins—the works. Don't leave out the male family members if they have a penchant for cooking, too. Many families include men who share the cooking chores, and often it's the man of the family who handles the barbecuing and outdoor grilling. If Uncle Jim has a great shortcut recipe for stew from his bachelor days, or Dad in his single days had a great way of making hash from a can taste special with a little doctoring up, include that, too.

If there's a story that goes with the recipe, by all means include it. Was this the dish Mom first cooked for Dad? Did Grandpa propose to Grandma over the Boeuf Bourgignon recipe she's providing? Was Uncle

Ted's Firehouse Chili recipe really prepared by firemen during his days as a firefighter? Is your daughter's
Franks'n'Beans recipe the one she makes herself whenever you're out for the evening, and the first thing she
ever learned to cook? That information should be included in the cookbook.

When you have at least one recipe (possibly many!)
from every family member who cooks, and you're sure
you've included all the family favorites and all the extra
special goodies, it's time to turn them into a book.

Arrange the recipes in the order you want them. Possible ways of organizing the book include separating
recipes by contributor or by family branch, separating
soups from meats from desserts, etc., or separating the
book into recipes kids can make, harder recipes, and
difficult specialites. If some other other order appeals
to you, by all means use it.

To make the pages of the book, fold typing paper
(8 ½ × 11″) in half, top to bottom, pressing hard on
the fold, and turn the paper sideways. The short ends
are now on the top and bottom, the long ends on the
sides. Type or print on the outer sides only. (In other
words, of four possible surfaces you could write on, you
are writing only on the outer two.) Leave a margin of
about ¾″ on the folded side and 1 ½″ on the unfolded
side, which is the side that is going to be bound. (The
folded edge will be the outer edge of each page in your
book. So when you are writing on each folded sheet of
paper, know that the side of the paper with the fold to
the right is the first page of that pair, and the overleaf,
the side of the paper with the fold to the left, is the
second page.)

If you organize the recipe book into a section for each
contributing family member, you may even want to leave
space for a photo of each person at the beginning of his
or her section.

When the pages are all written or typed, and in the

correct order, place all the unfolded edges neatly together and staple down the length of the pages, about ½″ in
from the edge.

To make the cover for the book, use rubber cement to
attach pretty wallpaper or fabric to the outside of each of
two pieces of cardboard. Leave about ½″ of excess fabric
on all sides. After the fabric is glued in place, make a
small diagonal cut across the corner of the excess fabric,
so it will fold squarely over the corners of the cardboard.
Then carefully glue it down.

Finally, glue a piece of heavy construction paper to
the inside of each cover, overlapping the edges of the
fabric.

If desired, you can cut fabric letters for the title, or
you can print it with waterproof ink on the fabric or
wallpaper.

The front and back covers are now complete, ready to
be attached to the book with a row of staples. Finish the
binding with wide cloth tape to cover the staples, and
your book is complete.

SIMON SAYS CLEAN YOUR ROOM

Materials needed: None

You probably remember the game Simon Says, and if
you have three or more kids, or your kids have company
over in wholesale quantities, you may even have played
the game with them. But did you know the game can be
used to motivate them to do chores such as clean up their
rooms?

But first, here's a refresher course for those of you
who haven't played Simon Says lately and can't quite
remember the rules. One person is Simon, and Simon
gets to give orders to the others: "Simon Says close your
eyes and stick your tongue out." "Simon says hop on
one foot." "Simon says squat down." Whatever Simon

says, they must do. But if Simon just says "Touch your toes" without saying "Simon says" first, and someone does it, they're out of the game. The last one out is the winner. Simon should bark out the orders quickly, not giving the players a chance to think, "Did s/he say 'Simon says'?"

Okay, now how do you turn this into a room-cleaning aid? To begin with, the kids are much more apt to clean their rooms if you turn it into a game, and if they are willing participants, you're much more likely to be willing, too—willing to stand there and give them specific instructions instead of just saying, "Clean your room up."

We all know that sometimes a child will look at a messy room, feel overwhelmed, and give up before even starting. Breaking the room down into specific chores makes it much easier, but usually that requires a little parental guidance.

Kids today are mostly too sophisticated to think they're playing a game just because you say, "Simon says clean your room up." But if you turn the project into a silly challenge, *then* there's an element of fun for them.

"Simon says stand on one leg while you put those books away." "Simon says put all the blocks away with your left hand—and keep your right hand up in the air the whole time." "Simon says to hop over to the closet to put your clothes away."

By turning the task into a challenge you involve the child in a game and in a situation where s/he wants to prove s/he *can* do whatever it is, instead of rebelling against being asked to clean her/his room. And by making it silly, you make it fun.

For that matter, you don't even have to play Simon Says. Sometimes, just for variety, give him or her silly challenges without playing Simon Says: "Bet you can't put all the blocks in front of you in the toy chest next to you with your eyes closed." "Do you think you can

clean the whole left half of your room on one foot
without putting your other foot down on the floor?"
"Bet you can't put away all the yellow blocks with
your left hand and all the red blocks with your right
hand without messing up at least once."

It won't work with every child every time, but it will
work with most kids often enough.

SING-ALONG

Materials needed: None

Mitch Miller had the right idea back in the seven-
ties—everybody likes to sing along. Whether you're a
two-person family or a ten-person family, you can sing
together while you do the dishes, while you're on a
drive (it eases the fidgets), or while you're not doing
anything else, but are just gathered in the living room
for the express purpose of singing together.

Any song the kids know will do, or pick one they
don't know but could learn easily, and teach them. Silly
songs can be the most fun for kids; popular favorites that
have been around for ages include "Bill Grogan's Goat,"
"Found a Peanut," and "There's a Hole in the Bucket."

Or try making up new words to an old, familiar
melody. Kids are great at that; what's sillier than a
five-year-old? One family I know took "Up on the
Housetop" and came up with the following: "Up on the
housetop, moans and groans/Listen to poor old Santa's
bones/Down through the chimney—stuck again/How he
wishes he were thin."

Singing—whether old favorites, newly learned songs,
or made-up songs—is just plain fun. And thinking up
new words for old songs promotes language development and creativity, and stretches the imagination. Don't
worry if the rhyme is a little flawed; you're not trying to
win a Grammy for this one. And if there's a flaw in the
meter? Who cares about the meter—this isn't a taxi!

JAM-BOREE

Materials needed: One quart fresh berries, 4 cups sugar, 1 pouch liquid pectin, 2 teaspoons lemon juice, 5 one-cup capacity plastic containers (you can use soft margarine or yogurt containers in lieu of buying specially made freezer containers)

Here's a fun project the family can get involved in together that will result in an edible product the kids will enjoy. Making homemade jams and jellies for your freezer is an activity even very young kids can help out with.

You can use berries you've picked in the wild yourself (see "Go Berrying," page 101), or if one is in your vicinity you can visit a farm where you can pick your own berries, which is more fun and less money than buying them in a store, or you can buy the berries at the farmers' market or supermarket.

The recipe here is for strawberry jam, since strawberries are available in most areas of the country. But if your tastes run in other directions, or if strawberries aren't available in your area, consult a cookbook and use another type of berry.

The family can all work together to clean the berries, sort out any bad ones from the batch, measure the one quart you'll need for each batch of jam, and then hull them.

When that's done, and the berries have been placed in a large bowl, add the sugar and lemon juice, stir, and set it aside for ten minutes. Then stir in the pouch (3 ounces) of liquid pectin, stirring constantly for three minutes. Now ladle the mixture into clean plastic containers and let it stand in them at room temperature for twenty-four hours. After that, store in the freezer till ready to use.

When the kids spoon the jam onto their toast, they'll be proud to be able to say, "We made it ourselves!"

HOMEMADE JUICE-SICLES

Materials needed: Any kind of fruit juice, small Dixie cups, aluminum foil or plastic wrap, Popsicle sticks

The kids will enjoy making their own Popsicle-type treats, and you'll enjoy knowing they're made from good juice, not sugar and water. All they have to do is pour any kind of juice into small Dixie cups, and for each cup make a Popsicle-stick-sized slit in a piece of aluminum foil or plastic wrap, cover the cup with the wrap, and insert the stick all the way down into the cup. Put the cups in the freezer and leave them there until they're solid.

Now you don't need to worry about healthy foods when the kids want ices—you can let them eat these treats and know they're getting good nutrition. (They can even eat 'em for breakfast!)

Making them is fun, too.

MAKE MOUNTAIN MUSIC

Materials needed: Any of the following: Comb and can or cup; rubber bands and small box; coffee can with plastic lid and beads, or beans, or empty wooden thread spools; pie tin and fork or spoon; washboard and wooden spoon

Any of the combinations listed above will provide a reasonable approximation of music, most appropriate to a family hillbilly band (see also "Family Band," page 72). A few explanations may be in order:

Play the comb by rubbing it against the side of the can or cup so its teeth grate against the edge. Stretch the rubber bands across the lidless box so they reverberate like guitar strings. Shake the coffee can, to rattle the beads, beans, spools, or whatever other small items you decide to use. Bang the pie tin with the fork or spoon. Drag the wooden spoon down the washboard to make a satisfying musical sound.

Sing along with the music. Traditional or country songs work best with this type of instruments. Surely your kids know "On Top of Old Smoky." Perhaps you know and can teach them "Sweet Betsy From Pike."

If the kids want to make a big production out of this activity, they can even dress country style. Any of the following will help: a checked and/or ripped flannel shirt; coveralls; a bandanna; an old skirt that can be turned into a granny dress; a ruffled blouse.

REACH OUT AND TOUCH SOMEONE

Materials needed: Paper, markers or crayons— and compassion

Surely there is a nursing home somewhere near you, and just as surely there are residents in it who not only have no one coming to visit them but no one even sending them mail, no one to brighten their days. Cheering them up is one of the kindest and most caring acts anyone can do. And the process can be enjoyable for a child when it involves a fun crafts project.

The crafts project in question is making individualized, custom-designed greeting cards. It's easy.

The child folds a piece of typing paper in half horizontally, then in half again, resulting in a greeting-card-sized arrangement. S/he draws whatever cheering picture comes to mind, perhaps with a greeting, an uplifting or friendly message, or just a brightly crayoned "Hello

from your friend————." You, the parent, can help
by suggesting appropriate sentiments or greetings for
the card.

The card may engender a response from the recipient,
which may result in an ongoing correspondence if the
child is interested. Or your child may prefer, rather than
entering into a correspondence with one nursing-home-
bound senior, to keep sending out cards from time to
time to different nursing home residents, sending a bit of
cheer into different corners and spreading some sunshine
where it's needed most.

A call or visit to any nursing home in your area will
provide you with a list of names of people who would
welcome, and be greatly cheered by, the arrival of such
mail. There are few more compassionate and genuinely
uplifting gestures, though two others follow.

ADOPT-A-GRANNY

Materials needed: Nothing but caring

In addition to sending cards to nursing home residents
(see above), your children may be interested in actually
visiting people who live in nursing homes. Again, the
operator of a local home can supply you with the names
of residents who don't have visitors. These may be
people with no living relatives, people with uncaring
relatives, or people whose family lives far away.

Your children may enter into a relationship with a
nursing home resident through sending cards of cheer
to her or him, or they may embark upon the relationship
without any prior introduction. Though some children,
especially younger ones, are put off by or frightened by
the appearance of a much older person, others—especially older ones less prone to unnecessary fear—jump
at the chance to do a good deed and make a difference
in someone's life.

This is especially suitable for kids who don't have grandparents of their own, or whose grandparents live out of the area, but even kids with four grandparents living within a mile of their homes can benefit from a relationship with an older person and the warm glow that comes from knowing they've truly enriched another person's life. And there's no such thing as having too many grandparents.

The nursing home visits don't have to be often, or of long duration. Even ten minutes once a month would mean a lot to an older person who lives in a nursing home and who gets no other visitors. The kids can each "adopt" a granny or grandpa, bringing her or him pictures they colored, crafts they've made, or a little treat like a candy bar, if the senior in question is not under dietary restrictions.

By encouraging your kids to engage in a relationship with someone whose lonely life will be enriched by the kids' visits, you're teaching them the truest act of charity—giving of themselves.

NOURISHMENT—PHYSICAL AND SPIRITUAL

Materials needed: Just time, energy, and caring— and an adult with a car

Your town almost certainly has a food bank, and your town's food bank certainly serves a painfully deep need. It's never too early for children to learn about those less fortunate, and to learn the importance of helping others. If your children belong to the Scouts, they may already be helping collect for a local food bank. If they don't belong to an organization that collects for the less fortunate, there's no reason they can't do it on their own. (And even if they do belong to such an organization, they can still do it on their own, too.)

Not only will they learn that people in need exist right here in America, not just in those newspaper pictures of starving children overseas, they will also learn the joy of helping others.

With an adult's help—and accompanied by an adult at least at the curb if not to each front door—the children can go from door to door, covering as large an area as is feasible, collecting one can of food (or one box of spaghetti or bag of noodles or bag of flour or bag of diapers) from each house, explaining that it's for the food bank.

You'll be astonished at how quickly you acquire a car full of staples, and at how quickly your child acquires an understanding of other people's need as well as a sense of pride in doing something truly meaningful and necessary for someone.

Deliver the bounty to the food bank, and go home fed spiritually by the knowledge that you've helped feed someone physically.

✂ Excursions

WHERE DOES MILK COME FROM?

Materials needed: None

Where does milk come from? Many kids ask their parents that question at some point or another, though some accept on blind faith that it comes from the supermarket,—and that's that. If asked, most of us explain about milk coming from cows, perhaps going into some detail, perhaps just letting it go at that. But there is more to it than the farmer milking the cow. Why not give the kids a look behind the scenes?

If you live within a reasonable drive of a working dairy farm that welcomes visitors, by all means take the kids and let them see the big milking machines, preferably when they're in operation, if the timing can be arranged. Some farms even allow hands-on participation. Again, depending on timing, the kids may have a chance to see 400-gallon tanks of milk being emptied into a refrigerated tanker.

Even if you live in a large metropolitan area, too far from a working farm, chances are you live near a milk bottling plant. Whether or not your kids can get a farm tour, by all means take them to tour the bottling plant. Let them see where the milk is pumped when it leaves the refrigerated tanker. Quite possibly it will go into a large silo.

Many plants specialize in one specific kind of milk production; for example, some make cheese, some make powdered milk or dry milk products, and some bottle whole milk. The kids may get the opportunity to see cottage cheese being processed, cream separated from milk, or milk bottles or even ice cream cartons being filled. (Did they ever think before about where ice cream comes from?) Perhaps there are several milk plants in your vicinity that specialize in different milk products. Visit them all.

The next time you take the kids to the supermarket, discuss the steps milk takes before it gets to the store. Remind them of the various processes it goes through, which they've seen. They might even be interested in a discussion of the number of different jobs there are for people in bringing milk from the cow to your kids' glasses.

There's the farmer (and all the people at the farm), the person who drives the milk truck to the processing plant, the various people the kids saw at the processing plant, the people who drive the milk to the supermarket, and all the people who work at the supermarket.

Less obvious are the veterinarian who takes care of the cows, the farmer whose farm grows grain to feed to the cows (probably a different farmer than the one who owns the cows), and even the people who build the tractors used on the farm where they grow the grain. How many others can your kids think of? This can lead into quite an introduction to economics at an elementary level.

If your kids got caught up in tracking milk from the dairy farm to the supermarket, there may be similar opportunities nearby. Why not track the origins of a loaf of bread, from grain growing in fields through a bakery and into the store? If you don't live near grain fields, at least you may live near a commercial bakery that offers tours.

Does fruit grow nearby? Will the packing plant allow

you and the kids to visit? What about a poultry farm, where eggs are produced? Do you live in an area where maple syrup is produced? Wouldn't the kids love to see where the syrup they pour on their waffles comes from?

Depending on where you live, the possibilities vary, but these behind-the-scenes tours are not only interesting to kids, they're instructive on a variety of levels.

FIT FAMILY FUN

Materials needed: Paper and pen; strollers for really young kids

Walking is an inexpensive—make that *free*—way to keep your family fit, and an activity that the whole family can participate in. It's never too early to get kids involved in fitness, though if a child is really young, you may want to bring along a stroller and plop him or her into it when his/her legs get too tired to walk farther.

Start out with a manageable distance, even if it's ridiculously easy for you; then increase that as the kids' legs get accustomed to the walk. Point out anything and everything you observe along the way; a walk is a good time to sharpen the kids' powers of observation.

Keep a chart of distances walked and the time it took; at the end of each week and month, tally the total mileage everyone has walked. You might be surprised at how many miles you walk in a month (or any other given period) once the kids work their way up to some serious walking.

You may even want to involve the kids in a walk-a-thon for your favorite charity. Just as it's never too early for them to learn fitness, it's never too early for them to learn to help others; and this is a way to accomplish that *and* stay fit and have fun, all at once.

AN "OBSERVATION" TOUR

Materials needed: None

Take a walk or drive through a neighborhood that's unfamiliar to your kids. A walk is better, though to get to an unfamiliar neighborhood you may have to pile into the car and drive a little distance.

Let everyone discuss what they see, hear, and even smell as they walk, and what they feel, if possible (the bark of unfamiliar trees, for instance). Taste may come up, too—we'll get to that later. This is not just an activity to pass time. The kids are learning to be observant and also to think and draw conclusions about what they observe.

What kinds of buildings are they observing? New houses, older houses, apartment houses, farms, stores, offices, industrial buildings? What can they tell you about the neighborhood from what they observe?

Assuming this is a residential neighborhood, how is it the same as the neighborhood where you live? How is it different? What conclusions can they draw from looking around? Listening? Smelling? Are the smells in this neighborhood different from your own neighborhood? Heavier cooking smells? Different flowers if flowers are currently blooming? What else can they smell? There may be an industrial neighborhood within sniffing distance, or a commercial bakery, or something else that smells different from your own neighborhood.

Are the houses bigger or smaller, the front yards bigger or smaller? Do the kids think the backyards are bigger to compensate, if the front yards are smaller? Or do they think the backyards match and are smaller, too?

If you live in a neighborhood of new houses, and these are older houses, how do they compare in other ways? Do they have all kinds of intricate designs, scrollwork, and other architectural features? Can the kids recognize that the architectural styles are different, even though they don't know the names of different styles of architecture?

Are the windows different? Do they slide from side to side, or open out, instead of sliding up and down? Or are they jalousies? Discuss the different types of windows that exist. The kids may have taken it for granted that all windows are like the windows you have at home. What about the doors? Are they plain or ornate? Are there screen doors or not? Can you spot any Dutch doors, in which the top half opens while the bottom stays closed? Did the kids even know there are such doors? Are there front porches here and not in your neighborhood?

What kind of mailboxes do you have at home—a mail slot in the front door, or an open-topped mailbox attached to the house, or a front-opening mailbox on a post right at the curb? Do the kids know mail can be delivered in these different ways? What kind(s) do you spot in this new neighborhood?

Do they hear unfamiliar sounds? Do they know what they are? Can they at least guess?

Do you live in a development or neighborhood of one-story homes? Are you walking around in a neighborhood of two-story homes now (or vice versa)? Discuss what differences that might make in the lifestyles of the people who live there. Does your home have a basement? Most do, but some don't.

If you don't live in Florida, do your kids know that most Florida homes don't have basements? (It's because the water table is so high, but if they're old enough to guess at that, don't tell them why, at first. Let them try to figure it out.) This is also true in other locations as well. (If you do live in Florida, do your kids know what a basement is?)

Discuss the differences in lifestyle created by having versus not having a basement. Where do people in houses without basements put their laundry rooms? Where do they store things? Do they have to keep fewer old possessions on hand due to reduced storage space? If they don't have basements in which to put playrooms, do they still have playrooms? You can really get the kids thinking about differing lifestyles with such discussions. They may even get their first realization that not all people live similar lifestyles.

Are the homes in the neighborhood you're touring well maintained? Are the lawns well tended, or do they look neglected? Are the houses themselves dilapidated or well kept up? Is there strewn trash or are the streets immaculate, or are conditions somewhere in between? Discuss the various possible causes. Some that the kids might think of for a neighborhood in disrepair might include: "The people are slobs." "There are lots of kids in the neighborhood to throw papers all over." "The ice cream truck comes by a lot." "The people work hard, maybe two jobs, and don't have enough time to keep the property up." "The people just don't care." "The people are renters and the landlords are cheap." "The houses are so old that they get into disrepair faster than the people can keep up with fixing them." "The people try hard, but they don't have enough money to keep up with necessary repairs." What other possible conclusions can they come up with? What other discussions can these conclusions lead to?

If you live on a well-traveled street and are touring a neighborhood of quiet streets, perhaps dead-end streets, do the kids recognize that children in this neighborhood can play in the street fairly safely instead of having to stay on the sidewalk?

If you are touring an industrial neighborhood, ask what conclusions the kids might draw about the kinds of industries found around there. Now is a good time to discuss the town or general area in which you live and the industries to be found there, as well as any natural resources. Is there a principal resource, principal industry, or principal product that your area is known for? Are the kids aware of it?

If the kids hear a factory whistle, do they know what it is? Discuss it with them, but before telling them what it is, if they don't know, let them first attempt to draw their own conclusions, however erroneous. Remember, this is not just a tour on which to learn things but a tour on which to learn to observe and draw conclusions.

If there are farms where you are touring, discuss what might be raised on that farm: Animals? Vegetables? Do the kids know that on some farms only animals are raised, and on some only vegetables, and on some both? Did they ever think about it before? Do they know what vegetables grow best in your area?

If you are in an unfamiliar neighborhood of stores, perhaps they will find a store whose window—or even whose smell—interests them. This aroma could be anything from pastry to leather. If you pass an ethnic food store or bakery, stop in and give your kids a taste of another land, even if it's pastry, and lunchtime is approaching. They can always take it home for after lunch.

There may be a large river or tiny brook in the neighborhood, giving you more things to observe and discuss. If this is a residential neighborhood, what differences would having a waterway in the neighborhood make to a person's lifestyle? If this is a commercial neighborhood, what advantage does having a waterway in the vicinity give to businesses in the area?

Now look at the street signs. Maybe all the streets in your area are named for trees. How are the streets you're touring named? If you find streets named after famous people, do the kids know who Jefferson, Franklin, Washington, or Lincoln are? Perhaps the streets are named after other types of famous people—writers or poets like Whitman, Browning, or Sandburg. Do those names have any meaning to the kids? If they're old enough to appreciate poetry, this trip could evolve into a trip to the library (see page 103) to borrow some of that poet's or writer's work.

If the streets in your own neighborhood are named after the developer's kids, or after scenic features like Sunset Lane, Morningside Avenue etc., and the neighborhood you're touring (whether residential, industrial, agricultural, or commercial) features streets that have the names of trees, let that be a springboard to a discussion of the different kinds of trees. How many can your kids name? (How many others can you supply for them after they've exhausted their knowledge?) Now try to find examples of as many as you can. If you're not sure which trees you see are which variety, go to the library to borrow a book on trees that identifies them by leaf.

If there is a park in the neighborhood, how does it differ from parks you have visited before? (You may even find an unexpected treat, like a unique playground with creative, different equipment.)

If you pass a statue or historical monument, ask the kids if they know anything about the person or event being commemorated. Before you tell them about the person, event, or whatever, let them guess. If the person in the statue is seated on a horse, for instance, what might that tell them about that person? Let them guess creatively—even if they're wrong—before you give them the real lowdown on who or what is being honored.

Another suggestion: If you live in the suburbs but not too far from a city, take a drive into the city and park in a residential neighborhood. Now take a tour around there. Chances are the houses are apartment buildings. If they're one-family houses, they may be built attached, with no space between them.

Discuss the differences in lifestyles between your family's life and these people's lives. Where do the kids play without a yard? What's it like to have neighbors upstairs and down? (Examples: You can't bounce a ball in the house. You can't yell secrets or the neighbors will hear.) Discuss all the things that might be different between your kids' lives and the lives of the kids who live on this street. Do they play different games? Are their schools likely to be nearer because there are more kids packed into a concentrated area? Are they more or less likely to walk to school rather than ride a school bus? Why? Might they ride a city bus rather than a yellow school bus? What do you suppose the kids do for fun after school? What other lifestyle differences are there likely to be?

If, on the other hand, you live in the city, drive out to the suburbs for a tour, and let the kids discuss the same types of questions, making all the observations they can about the possible differences in lifestyle.

Wherever you tour the kids should come away with four gains from the tour:

1. They will have a better knowledge of other neighborhoods.
2. They will learn to observe what's around them, and to use more than just their eyes. They should have been using their ears, their noses, their hands if there was anything they could touch, and even their sense of taste if you stopped into any unusual food shops.
3. They will have a better idea of how to draw a conclusion from what they observe.
4. They will have a better sense of how other people live if this was a tour of a residential neighborhood.

VIEW AN AIRSHOW

Materials needed: None

Call up your local hobby shop and ask when the next radio-controlled model airplane show is. Sure, buying and flying model airplanes can get pretty pricey, but going to view other people fly their planes is free.

Granted, the kids may want to own and fly their own planes, which definitely does not come under the heading of Free Family Fun, but you can always say no, and then again, they may not ask. They may be quite content to just watch the show.

VISIT THE POLICE STATION/FIREHOUSE

Materials needed: None

Most municipalities' fire departments and police departments are happy to give local residents a tour of their facilities. In some towns, these agencies schedule an open house once a year; in other locales, they welcome visitors any time there's not an emergency in progress. You should call ahead to find out what their policy is, and when you would be most welcome.

Many police departments include crime prevention tips and hand out flyers on safety, as part of the tour. At the firehouse, the kids may be allowed to climb on an engine, ring the bell, or tour part of the area where the firemen live when they're on duty. What's offered varies from one municipality to the next.

INTER-GENERATIONAL ANTIQUING

Materials needed: None

As an adult, you may have gone antiquing, but you may not have thought of bringing the kids. If you bring your parents (or, even better, your grandparents if they're alive and well and living nearby) along with you, the kids will have an even better time.

Why? Because some of the items you'll encounter on your expedition will be even more meaningful for your (or your spouse's) parents than to you, and can set them off on a series of remembrances. And you know how kids love to hear Grandma or Grandpa tell stories of the old days and how it was when Grandma and Grandpa were younger.

You don't have to *buy* anything when you go antiquing. Shop owners are quite used to browsers. Of course you might wind up acquiring a fabulous find, but you're more likely to acquire a bit of family history and leave with your checkbook intact.

Grandma, Grandpa, or Great-Gram can see an old toy and tell the kids (and you) how it was played with in their day, see an old piece of furniture and tell how Grandpa courted Grandma while sitting on a sofa or porch glider just like that one, see an old wash basin and tell the kids how wash was done in the old days. ("You mean you didn't have a washing machine?!" These stories can be real revelations to the kids.)

If the kids take an interest in the furniture and other objects themselves, that's great; but don't expect them to—the stories are what they're most likely to relate to. That's fine; you can enjoy the antiques while they're enjoying the stories. (But don't be surprised if *you* learn something from the stories, too—either a bit of family history that's new to you, or some information about how things were done in Grandma's time that even you weren't aware of.)

If your kids don't have a grandma or grandpa living nearby, invite an older neighbor to go along on the expedition instead.

GO BERRYING

Materials needed: Container(s) to carry berries in

Wild berries are fun to pick. If you and your kids live in a city, or the urbanized suburbs, they may never have seen berries growing, yet the odds are they're there, growing wild within a short drive from you. And even if you live in the suburbs or the country, the kids may never have gone berrying.

It's an enjoyable way to spend time together. How much time you spend will depend on your kids' patience, on how good the berrying is that day, and on how many berries your family can realistically consume (or has freezer space for). There's no sense in picking so many that bucketfuls will go to waste.

Most areas of the country are endowed with some kind of berries (or other wild fruit): Maine is known for blueberries, the Northwest has huckleberries, and the Washington coast has blackberries. There are cranberries, gooseberries, elderberries, and the list goes on. Strawberries are abundant in many parts of the country.

If you're not sure what berries grow in your part of the country and where to find them, check with your local County Extension Agent or the Department of Agriculture. This is especially important if you're not familiar with your local berries, as there are poisonous wild varieties.

The advantage to carrying one or two large pails is that there are fewer to carry. On the other hand, a larger quantity of smaller pails enables each kid (and parent) to carry his/her own pail, and with smaller quantities of berries, the ones on the bottom are less likely to get crushed.

If you find you've picked more berries than you can use quickly, freeze some by rinsing and draining them, then packing them loosely into plastic bags or margarine tubs, then sprinkling a few tablespoons of sugar over the top of each bag or tub and freezing it. You can also make jam (see "Jam-Boree," page 85) or bake pies.

If you do store berries in the freezer during the summer, when winter rolls around you can reach into your freezer and pull out a bag of sunshine.

A TRIP TO THE LIBRARY

Too many kids today are unfamiliar with that wonderful storehouse of treasures, the public library. Much has been said and written about today's kids not spending enough time reading, but even among families where books are abundant, not all kids are familiar with the library.

Libraries are great places on a lot of levels. Many libraries have programs geared to introducing kids to the library and keeping them coming back. Call your local library to see if they have read-aloud story hours for small children, films for kids of different ages, or other programs of interest to kids the ages of yours. Then take the kids and visit the *real* magic kingdom.

Don't just visit at times when there are special programs being offered. Take the kids to the library at other times, show them the vast array of books, and let them see for themselves what a treasure trove a library is. Let them browse among the selection of books—perhaps gently guided by you—and select books they'd like to sit and read or have you read to them right there (short picture books for little kids), or books to check out and take home.

If they're old enough, get them their own library cards. Can anything beat the sense of power a child feels when he or she first acquires a library card in his/her own name and can borrow any books he or she wants, up to the library's limit, and take them home to savor?

For slightly older kids, your trip to the library may include an explanation of how to use the card catalogue— which may be actual cards or microfilm or computerized. If you, yourself, don't know how to use a newer card catalogue, shed your embarrassment and let the librarian explain the system to you and your kids together. They'll be a jump ahead on future school research projects if they know how to use the card catalogue and access the library's vast resources.

Your library probably has a music collection, too. Whether your kids are into kiddie music or rock, the library is likely to have something they'd like to borrow. And now's a good chance for them to investigate a new type of music. Almost definitely the library has types of music they're unfamiliar with, possibly records or tapes or CDs in a category you don't have in your own collection, which the kids are unaccustomed to hearing. This might be their chance to get hooked on folk music or even ethnic music.

And if they're not real little ones and can be left to browse among the stacks for a few minutes, set a good example and look into the books for adults. When's the last time you borrowed a library book?

ROCK ON!

Materials needed: Rocks (to be collected nearby), borrowed library book

Here's another expedition that in part involves a trip to the library (see page 103). Take the kids out—in your backyard, if you live in a house rather than an apartment; in a nearby park, whether or not you live in a house; at the shore, if you live near the ocean or a lake; and anywhere else that seems a likely place for collecting rocks.

Each child should try to find at least one of as many different kinds of rocks as s/he can. But don't restrict the kids to just one, if they find several examples of one type that they find particularly pretty or interesting. Wash them all carefully when you get them home. (The rocks, that is, not the kids—though the kids may need it, too!)

Now, assuming they don't already own a book describing and illustrating the different kinds of rocks there are, go to the library and take one out. Identify all the rocks you've collected. See what kinds are missing from everyone's collection. Are they found in your part of the country? Let the kids all keep their eyes open for the missing examples their collection needs to be as complete as possible. In fact, you can go on periodic expeditions in search of the missing types of rocks needed to complete their individual collections, a worthwhile purpose for future family outings.

BE A TOURIST AT HOME

Materials needed: None

It's axiomatic that many, if not most, New Yorkers have never been to the Statue of Liberty or the observation floors of the Empire State Building (even if they work in that building). Similarly, people who live in or near most fair-sized to large cities have not availed themselves of its tourist attractions.

You've probably taken the kids to the nearest zoo, but is there a botanical garden, museum, historical landmark, or other tourist site nearby? Probably there are quite a few, and the odds are that at least some of them would be of interest to your kids. But I'll bet you haven't seen them all. There's also a good chance that some of these locations are open to the public at no cost, at low cost, or for a discretionary contribution.

Don't let the suggested contribution—if there is such a suggestion made—cow you into feeling you *have* to contribute that much. Take it as what it's called: a suggestion. If that amount times the number of people in your family is more than your budget can comfortably afford, pay what you comfortably can and no more.

Find out if your city, or the city you live near, has

a tourists' bureau or visitors' bureau, and contact them to request a brochure of tourist attractions. Chances are you'll find some places listed that you never heard of, or at least never thought of taking the kids to. Think again.

The kids may be a year older than they were the last time you discarded the thought of taking them to a particular attraction. They may be studying something in school this year that would make a visit to a particular museum more meaningful or relevant. They're older now, more interested in a wider spectrum of things, more able to tour a museum without fidgeting.

So read the tourist brochures, look over descriptions of tourist attractions you weren't already aware of, and reconsider the ones you'd rejected before instead of mentally discarding the idea just because you had done so previously.

Get out there and play tourist.

✂ Active Games and Activities

KNOWLEDGE TAG

Materials needed: None

The premise of basic tag, of course, is that everyone runs away from one player, who is it, and chases the others. Depending on house rules, these other players may or may not have to remain within certain boundaries. When the player who is it succeeds in tagging another player, s/he yells, "Tag—you're it," and this other player now becomes it and chases all the others.

Stoop Tag (which really should be called Squat Tag, because the players are squatting, not stooping) is a variation in which, if you squat down before it touches you, it cannot tag you.

But there is a variation on Stoop Tag, in which a player cannot simply squat to get away from it. S/he must also call out a name/word in a certain category, and it must be one that has not been used before in this round. For instance, for Indian Tag, a player who squats must simultaneously yell out the name of a Native American tribe, a tribe that has not already been used this round. If s/he fails to yell out a legitimate, previously unused tribe name as s/he squats, the squat doesn't count and it can tag him/her. In State Tag, it is state names that are called out. In Country

Tag it is countries of the world. In Author Tag it's writers.

In my childhood, we often used such esoteric categories as fabrics and medicines; you, the parent, may wish to steer the categories to those requiring knowledge of a more educational value, but there's nothing wrong with letting the kids choose their own, less educational categories such as cartoon characters or TV shows.

And, parents, there's no reason you shouldn't join in the game. Of course, if the kids choose to play Cartoon Tag, there's an excellent chance you're going to spend an awful lot of time being it!

MARBLE ROLL

Materials needed: Empty can, marble, possibly chalk, possibly paper and pen or pencil for keeping score if desired

A discarded can with the lid completely removed is the target at which you'll roll a marble. The can should have been thoroughly washed and dried and examined for possible sharp spots left by the can opener. If there are protruding sharp spots, discard it and try another can.

Lay the can on its side, with the open top facing you. Roll the marble at the can from behind an agreed-upon line, perhaps at a distance of three feet. (This can be adjusted according to the ages and skills of the players.) Since the marble has to go into the can, and the can is not absolutely flat to the ground, due to its thickness, this is not as easy as it may sound. A slight skipping motion of the marble helps, rather than a smooth roll. But too much skip and the marble will roll off course. You may find that the kids are better at this than you parents are!

This is not a good game to play on a carpet; if playing indoors, a smooth tile, linoleum, or even wood floor is a preferable playing surface, rather than a carpet or rug. If playing outdoors, the smoother the concrete or asphalt the better, though an uneven surface will add challenge to the game.

After a few practice rolls for every player, which will give them a feel for how to best roll the marble, you'll have a better idea of how good your family is at this and will be able to set a reasonable goal that someone can reach in an amount of time that won't try the patience of the players. If you find that they're scoring easily, make twenty "baskets" the winning score. If they're all finding it difficult, set an easier goal, like seven. Whoever scores that many "baskets" first, wins the game.

You can also make the game easier or harder to win by adjusting the distance between the can and the line from behind which the players are rolling the marble. Indoors this can be a certain square on the tile floor or spot on the linoleum or plank of wood. Outdoors it can be a crack in the pavement or a line drawn with chalk.

You can keep count in your heads or write the score down on paper (or with chalk, on the pavement, if playing outdoors) to avoid disputes ("I had six." "No you didn't; you only had five.").

DRY-LAND FISHING

Materials needed: Large pan (such as dishwashing pan or roasting pan) or wastebasket, sticks or twigs (about a foot long) or rulers, string, bobby pins, hole punch, paper or (preferably) cardboard, scissors, possibly crayons or markers or paint

The first order of business is to create the fish. The kids can cut them out of paper, but cardboard is better. They can be any size from about two inches long to about six inches long, and making them of varied sizes is preferable. If the kids want to, they can draw them first, then cut along the lines they've drawn. If your kids are all small, you may need to do this part yourself; if they're older, they'll enjoy cutting the fish out. The more fish the kids cut out, the more fun they can have catching them.

Then, if they want, they can color the fish, drawing eyes and mouths, gills and fins. Since these are not real fish, the colors don't have to be realistic. The kids can feel free to make them orange with green zigzags or pink with purple polka dots, if that's the kind of fish they want to go fishing for. Somewhere around each fish's mouth, make a hole with a hole punch.

Each child needs one stick, which will be his/her fishing pole, to which will be tied one length of string, perhaps a foot long. At the other end of the string, tie a bobby pin or hair pin that has been pried apart, with the tip of one end bent slightly. This is the hook on the fishing rod.

Now dump all the fish in the pan. Ideally, some of the fish will be on top of other fish, and they won't all be flat on the bottom of the pan. Some will be tilted upward, making it easier to catch them.

All the "fishermen" have to do is hook a bobby pin through the hole-punched mouth of a fish, keep it on the bent part of the pin, and extract it from the pan (this is not as easy as it sounds), and they've caught a fish.

This is one fishing expedition on which nobody will catch cold, fall in the water, or get mosquito-bitten, though you won't be able to eat the catch, either. But you can save the fish to throw back in the pan and catch over and over.

SHEET-BALL

Materials needed: Old sheet that can be cut up, scissors to cut it with, ball, clothesline or rope

This one's real simple: Just cut a hole in the sheet and hang it from a clothesline, if you have one in your backyard, or string a rope between trees and hang it from that. Then have the players stand behind an agreed-upon line and take turns trying to throw the ball through the hole in the sheet. Each successful throw earns a point. The first player to get 10 points (or any other number you agree upon ahead of time) is the winner.

If you have kids of widely differing ages playing, or if you parents are playing with the kids, you can make the game fairer for the younger players in either or both of two ways:

1. Draw two lines in the dirt (or with chalk on pavement), one farther back than the other. Have the older players stand behind the farther-back line, and the younger players behind the nearer line.
2. Cut two different holes in the sheet, a larger hole lower down on the sheet, and a smaller hole higher up on the sheet. The younger kids can aim for the larger, lower hole, which will be easier for them to get the ball through. The older kids or adults have to aim for the smaller, higher hole, which will be harder to score through.

HIT THE CLOWN

Materials needed: Large piece of scrap lumber, paint or chalk, bells or old bicycle horn or other noisemaker, possibly string or thread, heavy-duty stapler or nails, and beanbags (see Beanbag Toss, page 124)

This one's especially fun for the younger set. It serves a double purpose: They can have enjoy throwing something at someone—a picture of a clown, in this case—which is not only great fun but also great for getting out their aggressions. And they also get to make lots of noise.

The idea is simply to toss beanbags at a picture of a clown to which you've attached a noisemaker. By hitting the noisemaker, the kids succeed in make a satisfying noise. There is no winner or loser, just fun for all.

The target is a picture of a clown's face. On a piece of scrap wood, paint the picture or draw it with chalk, preferably chalk of different colors. The larger the piece of wood, the larger your picture, and the larger the better. The kids may have as much fun painting or drawing the clown's face as they will throwing the beanbags.

If you have an old bicycle horn, the type activated by squeezing a bulb to make a satisfying *honk*, use it for the nose, fixing it in place with nails. In the absence of a bicycle horn, give the clown earrings made of old bells. (Little Christmas-package jingle bells will do fine.) Attach each of the bells to a short length of string or thread, and staple or nail the other ends of the thread or string to the clown's ears. Lacking jingle bells, scout around the house to find anything else that makes a satisfying jingle, honk, rattle, or other noise, which you can attach to the clown's hat, collar, or other appropriate location.

If you don't already have beanbags, you can make them, following the directions given under "Beanbag Toss" (page 124).

Now all the kids—and you, if you're joining in—have to do is stand a reasonable distance back from the wood, take aim at the clown, and throw the beanbags, trying to honk the horn, ring the bells, or whatever.

HUNGRY CLOWN

Materials needed: Large piece of scrap lumber, saw, sandpaper, paints or chalk, beanbags

This is similar to "Hit the Clown," above, and is an old familiar carnival game. You, the parent, need to saw a hole in the lumber. The hole should be large enough to toss a beanbag through, and should be sanded around the edges to eliminate the hazard of splinters. Now have the kids use paints or chalk to draw a clown face around the hole, which is the clown's open mouth.

The object is to toss beanbags into the clown's open mouth. If you don't already have beanbags, you can make them, following the directions given under "Beanbag Toss" (page 124).

Everyone stands behind a line and tosses his or her beanbag at the clown's open mouth, trying to get the beanbag through the hole. The first player to do it five times wins the game. The beanbag must pass completely through the hole, not just rest on the lip.

If your kids are of widely diversified ages, you can make the game fairer for the little ones by having them stand nearer the target for their throws than the older kids, and in turn you parents can stand even farther back than the older kids.

SAFE PITCH 'N' BAT SET

Materials needed. Thick section of newspaper, tape, several mismatched socks

At last—a use for those socks whose mates have disappeared into that great void that must exist in everyone's sock-hungry washer and dryer (or whose mates have gotten holes in them). Roll several of them up to make a ball of them. Then roll up a thick section of newspaper and tape it together. You now have a bat.

Little ones too young to handle a regulation baseball or softball bat, and too young to pitch and catch a baseball or softball, can pitch and bat with this bat and ball with no fear of slammed fingers or of accidentally flung bats hurting another player. And these homemade bats and balls are a good budgetary alternative to lightweight store-bought balls and bats.

Batter up!

GOOFY GOLF

Materials needed: Newspaper bat and sock-ball (see "Safe Pitch 'n' Bat Set," above), blocks or any other suitable objects with which to delineate "goals" to drive the ball through in lieu of holes to sink the ball into

Since you don't want to dig holes in your backyard, this game of golf involves driving the ball between markers rather than sinking it into holes. How many markers you'll set up will depend on how many blocks or similar suitable objects you have lying around and how large your backyard is.

The rolled-up newspaper that serves as a bat in the "Safe Pitch 'n' Bat Set" (above) will become a golf club for this game, and the sock-ball from that set is your golf ball. Set up the blocks in pairs, leaving room between each pair to drive a sock-ball through it. Set the pairs up a suitable distance from each other. The distance should be defined by the ages of the players and the size and configuration of your backyard.

Each player takes a turn playing the first hole, keeping track of the number of strokes it takes him or her to drive the sockball through the space between the blocks. If the ball goes beyond the blocks without going through it, s/he must hit the ball back to the other side of the blocks and try again. When s/he has finally succeeded in driving the ball through the blocks, write down the number of strokes it took. Now it is the next player's turn.

When all players have played one hole, the first player sets the ball down just past the first hole and starts hitting toward the second. The others play in turn after the first player has driven the sock-ball through the blocks.

When all players have played all holes, the player with the lowest total score is declared the winner.

BASKETBUBBLES

Materials needed: Bubble-making liquid (commercial or homemade—see "Soap Bubbles," page 61), bubble wand (commercial or improvised, such as wire bent in circular shape or old pair of eyeglass frames without lenses), bucket or wastebasket

There are at least three variations on this activity, for one child or more.

Basic one-person activity: Get six or eight feet away from the bucket and blow a bubble. Your objective is to maneuver the bubble into the bucket with your breath alone, without touching the bubble with your fingers, the bubble wand, or anything else. After blowing the bubble, blow at the bubble to move it toward the bucket. If it starts to sink, you need to get under it and quickly blow upward to keep it from hitting the ground. But blow carefully so you don't send it in an entirely wrong direction away from the bucket at the same time. When it gets above the bucket, you may need to get above it and blow down, to land it right in the bucket and not have it drift out or land on the rim and break. This isn't as easy as it may sound. See how many bubbles you can land in the bucket.

Variation #1, for two players: One player tries to blow bubbles into the bucket, while the opposing player uses his/her breath to try to blow the bubbles away from the bucket. Then the players reverse roles, with the person who was opposing the bubbleblower now blowing the bubbles and the other person becoming the windy opposition.

Variation #2, for two or more players: Each player has his or her own wand, and a jar or dish of bubble solution. Each player has to see how many baskets s/he can score within a given number of minutes. The winner is the one who scores the most baskets in that time.

MILK JUG BALL TOSS

Materials needed: One empty plastic 1-gallon milk jug (or plastic water jug) per player, tennis ball or rubber ball, knife to be used by parent to cut milk jugs

You need to cut the milk jugs approximately in half, discarding the bottoms and retaining the tops. Each player holds one milk jug top upside down, by the handle, so the open end is up. Start with the ball in someone's jug. S/he makes a quick upward, outward movement with the jug, which tosses the ball up into the air and toward another player. This player now attempts to catch the ball in his or her jug. If successful, s/he now tosses the ball to the next player.

This is a cooperative game of catch, rather than a competitive game. It's hard enough to do, and that's where the challenge lies, rather than in one player challenging another. Two or more can play. If there are more than two, they stand in a circle. The ball can be tossed around the circle, in order, or across the circle at random.

GO FLY A KITE!—AND MAKE IT YOURSELF

Materials needed: Lightweight but sturdy paper, such as strong wrapping paper that is colorful, or plain paper that the child can decorate; two lightweight pieces of wood (such as balsa wood); large ball of string; material for a tail (such as an old tie, or several small rags knotted together); glue

Of course you can always go out and buy a kite, if you and your kids are all thumbs, or if your frustration tolerance is low, but making the kite can be half the fun and it's certainly much less expensive. With luck, you'll have all the items you need at home; if not, you won't need to buy much or spend much.

Glue the wood into crosspieces in traditional kite fashion (T-shaped) or attach the two pieces by holding them against each other in a T-shape and winding string around the cross connection over and over until the T is firmly connected.

One way to attach the paper is to make a notch across each of the four ends of the two pieces of wood and run one piece of string around through all four notches in a diamond shape. Now glue the paper onto the string. Attach the tail near the bottom of the longer piece of wood (the piece that will be vertical). Attach the string right at the juncture of the two pieces of wood. You now have a rudimentary kite.

Now all you need is a breezy day and an open space *away from electrical wires!* If the kite doesn't fly right, and you don't think the problem lies with the wind or the skill of the navigator, try adjusting the position and/or length of the tail, or try a heavier, lighter, longer, or shorter tail.

HOPSCOTCH

Materials needed: Chalk to draw the playing field with, a flattish rock or similar object to throw as your playing piece. (Everyone can use the same playing piece or each can have his/her own if desired)

Hopscotch is an old, old game for two or more players, largely favored by girls, which isn't played as much in these days of electronic games. That's too bad. It's a fun game, an outdoors game, a game that gets kids off their rears and doing something mildly physical. And there's no reason boys can't play, too.

You can play hopscotch in the city or the suburbs, or in the country if there's pavement around to draw the playing field on. It doesn't matter whether you live in an apartment or a house. City kids have been drawing hopscotch playing fields on the sidewalks in front of their apartment buildings for many generations, and of course suburban dwellers can draw the game field on their sidewalks or driveways, too.

You draw the squares in the following manner:

Draw one square and write a 1 in it. The size of the square should be roughly a little larger than the area your two feet would occupy if you were standing in it, which translates to approximately one foot by one foot unless all the players are very young with really small feet. Now draw another square, the same size, right next to it, and draw a 2 in that square.

Centered directly above those two squares, draw another the same size and label it 3. Above the 3 square, side by side, draw the 4 and 5 squares, parallel to the 1 and 2 squares, and above the 4 and 5 draw the 6, centered, parallel to the 3.

The 7 and 8 go side-by-side again, and the 9 completes the field, at the top. Some people draw the 9 as a semicircle rather than a square.

Your playing piece will probably be a flattish rock (flat so it doesn't roll much), though some city kids in olden days used squashed tin cans. Almost anything is acceptable that will fit comfortably in the players' hands, won't roll much, and has a comfortable weight. (Too light and it will bounce a lot; too heavy and you can't throw it comfortably.)

Standing behind the line that forms the bottom of the 1 and 2 squares, the first player throws or drops the stone or other playing piece (also known as a pottsy, from which comes the other name for Hopscotch, Pottsy) into the 1 square. If the stone lands in another square or rolls or bounces into another square, in other words, if it doesn't land fully within the borders of the square, the player's turn is over. If s/he successfully throws the stone within the 1 square, s/he now has to retrieve it in the following manner:

The player hops on one foot into the 2 square, the 3 square, the 4 square, and so on up to 9, then wiggles or hops around till s/he's facing in the other direction and hops back down again till s/he's standing in the 2 square. At no time may her/his foot touch a line or land in a wrong square. At no time may her/his other foot touch the ground. At no time until the player retrieves the stone may her/his hand touch the ground.

While standing in the 2 square, s/he retrieves the stone

from the 1 square using one hand only. If her/his other hand touches the ground for balance, her/his turn is over. After picking up the stone and standing straight again— still on one foot—s/he hops out of the playing field. S/he must get clear of the field with this hop, not landing on a line or partly in a square.

Having successfully completed "onesies," the player is now "for twosies." Now s/he must toss the stone into the 2 square. Again, it must land and stay fully within the square. If it bounces or rolls out, or touches the line, his/her turn is over.

This time s/he needs to hop on one foot into the 1 square and from there into the 3 square, skipping over the square the stone is in. (If s/he does hop into the 2 square, her/his turn is over.) From the 3 s/he proceeds from square to square up to the 9 and back again, this time stopping at the 3 square to retrieve the stone. The stone is always retrieved from the square numerically just above the square it's in, except for ninesies, when the stone is retrieved from the 8 square.

From the 3 square s/he hops to the 1 square (bypassing the 2, where the stone was), and from 1 s/he hops clear of the playing field. Now s/he's for threesies and throws the stone into the 3 square, going through the same procedure, and retrieving the stone while standing on one foot in the 4 square, then hopping from 4 to 2 to 1 and out.

Any time the player fails to comply with the rules, her/his turn ends and it becomes the next player's turn. As a player progresses farther up the playing field, it becomes increasingly harder to get the stone to land in the right square. Turns pass quickly from player to player.

Some people play that the game is over when the first person has successfully completed ninesies. That player is then declared the winner; others play that after ninesies, the players proceed backward, throwing into the 8, the 7, the 6 and so forth, until they're for "onesies back," and the first player to complete onesies back is the winner.

Another variation, mostly for younger players, allows players to land on two feet in the side-by-side squares, provided their playing piece is not in one of those squares. In other words, on onesies the player would hop with one foot into 2 and then 3 but could land with one foot in 4 and the other foot in 5, then hop one-footed into 6 and then land with one foot in 7 and the other in 8. Then the player would hop one-footed into 9 and either hop or wiggle around, jumping back into 7 and 8 with two feet again, and so on.

Parents, do you remember playing this as a child, or were you too busy watching television? For sure, your parents—at least, your mothers—played it. Get out there and play Hopscotch with your kids. I'll bet they can beat you. (And won't they enjoy that!)

THROW YOUR MONEY AROUND

Materials needed: Empty coffee cans (one for each player), coins (same assortment for each player)

This is a simple game for two or more kids, who'll enjoy both the competitiveness of the game and the *clink* as the coins land in the coffee can. Besides being fun as well as good practice in motor skills, it's also a good way for little kids to learn the value of the individual coins— a penny is worth one cent; a dime is worth ten cents, or the equivalent of ten pennies or two nickels, etc.

Each player stands the same distance from his or her can (a reasonable distance to be determined in advance by the parent), and each throws all of his or her coins, one at a time, at the cans. When all the coins have been tossed, each player counts the money in his or her can, and the winner is the person with the most money (in value, not in number of coins) in his or her can.

Variation for smaller children: Throw only pennies, so the only counting necessary is "one-two-three-four" (which will help them learn to count, if they need practice, even though they aren't learning the different denominations of coins, which can come later).

This variation also avoids fights over "I threw more coins in my can than she did. It's not fair that she won." (The winner threw in two quarters and got a score of fifty cents, beating the complainer who landed five pennies and two dimes, for a score of twenty-five cents, losing even though he got five more coins in the can than his sister.)

PENNY LAG

Materials needed: Coins, uncarpeted floor to play on. Optional: Paper and pen or pencil

Find a marker about ten feet from the wall. There may be a prominent board in the wood floor or line in the linoleum or tile, or you can put down a piece of tape or a shoe to mark the starting line. Each player stands behind that line to pitch coins at the wall. The winner is the one whose coin lands the nearest to the wall.

Each round can be a game unto itself, or the players can keep score round by round, marking down one point for a player each time s/he wins a round, with the winner of the game being the first one to get ten points, or the one who's ahead after fifteen tosses or at 5:30 or when Mom says dinner's ready.

To prevent any arguments over whose coin it is that's closer ("That's my quarter!"—"No, it's mine!"), kids can toss different denominations, with one child tossing a penny, another a dime, another a nickel, and another a quarter. If that causes dissension ("Your coin bounces better than mine! No fair!"), a different, small nailpolish mark on each penny can allow everyone to use the same type of coin and settle the squabbles.

Variation #1: Each child is given one of each denomination of coin, all the kids toss all their coins (one by one, of course), and a point is awarded for the nearest penny, the nearest nickel, the nearest dime, and the nearest quarter.

Variation #2: A circle is made of string—or several concentric circles are made of string—and the kids stand behind a line and aim their coins for the bull's-eye, getting a point if they land a coin in the circle. Or if there are two concentric circles, a point for landing in the outer circle, three points for the inner circle. (This variation can be played on carpet as well as wood, linoleum, or tile.)

This game—the basic game or either of the variations—can of course be played outdoors in good weather, with any wall, curb, stoop, or board used as the goal, or with chalk circles being drawn on the sidewalk or driveway, or string laid down on the grass for the bull's-eye version.

NICKEL GOLF

Materials needed: One coin per player. (Having different denominations for each player can help prevent arguments about just whose nickel is hovering on the lip of the cup)

For this game for two or more players, the kids will need your permission to make a couple of indentations in the lawn. They need one indentation about the size of a teacup, which they can make by digging the heel of a shoe into the turf and turning in a circle, and a lag line, or starting line, about fifteen feet away, that's made by scratching with a heel.

The players stand behind the lag line, and each tosses his or her coin underhand toward the hole. Players play in turn; after each player has tossed, the first player goes to where his or her coin is, picks it up, and tosses it again. The object, of course, is to land the coins in the hole.

There are two ways to score this. One is to play a prearranged number of rounds, keeping track of how many tosses it takes each player to get the coin in the hole. At the end of the agreed-upon number of rounds, the player with the lowest score wins, as in golf.

The other is that the first player to land his/her coin in the hole wins the round, and the players all go back to the starting point to play another round. Winner can be the best score after ten rounds, or the first player to score ten (or fifteen, or five, or whatever number is agreed upon ahead of time).

It's fairest to rotate who's first to toss: the player who wins one round can be the first to toss in the next round, or the loser can have the opportunity to toss first next time, or everyone can have a turn, starting with the oldest or with the youngest.

Variation: Instead of tossing the coins, roll them. This takes longer and isn't good for kids with low frustration tolerance. It also isn't good for families with tall grass.

BEANBAG TOSS

Materials needed: For the beanbags: Squares of scrap material, filler such as beans, lentils, or seeds, or nut shells, or packaging "popcorn." For the targets: Shoe boxes or any other boxes of a similar size and depth

Beanbag toss is an old game that's still fun. If you have small beanbags already in the house, great! If not—and they're not as common as they used to be—they're easy to make from the materials listed above. For the squares of scrap material you can cut up old sheets, cleaning rags that don't have holes in them, sections of worn-out kids' clothes, or use scrap material from clothes you've made at home if you're a sewing machine whiz.

A good size for a beanbag is 3″ × 3″, but if your scraps lend themselves to a different size beanbag, that's fine, too. Turning the material inside out, sew it on three sides. If you have a sewing machine, it's so much easier, but if not, you can do it by hand. Since beauty is not an object here, any child old enough to use a needle respectfully is old enough to join in on sewing, and every family member can sew his/her own beanbag and take pride of craftsmanship. Sewing the beanbags can itself become an activity to take part in productively.

After the beanbags are sewn on three sides, turn them right-side-out and stuff them good and full with the filling, using any of the items suggested above or anything else suitable you may have around the house. If you have a pillow you're about to discard, the feathers, foam, or other filling from the pillow can be removed and used as beanbag stuffing, too. Now sew up the fourth side of the beanbags, and you're ready to lay out the targets. Fine stitching is not necessary; just remind the kids to get the stitches tight enough that the filling won't come out, especially if you're using small beans or seeds.

The targets are the shoe boxes or other similar-size boxes. In the bottom of each shoe box, write a value: the number of points it's worth to land a beanbag in that box. If the boxes are not of equal size, lay them out in a straight line next to each other, and assign a higher point value to a smaller, harder-to-hit box, a lower point value to a larger, easier-to-hit box. If the boxes are of equal sizes, which is better, lay them out with each one successively farther away from the throwing line than the one before it, and assign the highest value to the box you place farthest away from the throwing line, and a lower value to each successively nearer box.

Exactly how many boxes you use will depend in part on how many of them you have lying around the house and also on how young or old, skilled or unskilled your family members are. If you have four boxes, try that number the first time. Set each a little farther away from the starting line. You may want to experiment before- hand, having your youngest child throw the beanbag as far as s/he can toss it, as a guideline to where to place the boxes.

For indoor play, it's a good idea to restrict the throws to underhand only. For outdoor play, you may want to give the little ones a handicap by allowing them to toss overhand if they wish and restricting parents, and possibly older kids, to underhand throws.

The first time you play, mark your nearest (or largest) box 5, and the others 10, 15, and 20 (for the farthest, or smallest). After you've played once, you can adjust your scoring in accordance with your family's skill. The first player to reach 100 wins; again, this is adjustable, so that if your family reaches 100 quickly, you can make 200 the winning number instead; or if they frustrate easily, and it seems to take forever for somebody to reach 100, make 50 the winning score.

Everyone has to stand behind a line to throw, but if you wish, you can have one starting line for the kids and a different line for the adults. You can draw the line with chalk if you're playing outdoors, or lay down a piece of string in a straight line for indoors play. Or use the time-honored imaginary line: Throw from behind an imaginary line from the left front foot of the chair over to the table, or an imaginary line from that tree root to the tall dandelion.

Since this game can be played indoors as well as out— as long as you have a room where it's safe to toss the beanbags without jeopardizing lamps, knicknacks, and other valuables—it's great for a rainy day. If you don't have a playroom, your living room isn't beanbag-proof, and the kids' rooms are too small, consider playing in the hall!

BABY BOX-BUGGY

Materials needed: Sturdy coardboard box or carton with sides tall enough to come up to a baby's armpits

The essence of simplicity, this brief pastime proves that kids don't need fancy, expensive toys to keep them occupied. For this you need one cooperative baby who's old enough to sit up well, and one strong older brother or sister (or mom or dad). A blanket tucked around the baby may help to stabilize the little passenger.

All you do is seat the baby in the box and push or pull the box along the floor, but of course if you wish to add sound effects (toot-toot, chugga-chugga-chugga, puff puff, or brrrrrrmmmm), well, that just adds to the fun.

That's all there is to it—proving that expensive baby toys, while they have their place, aren't an absolute necessity in this world. The game is over when the baby gets bored or, more likely, when the older sibling (or parent) gets tired.

BOBBING FOR APPLES

Materials needed: Very large pan, such as deep roasting pan, or large plastic dishpan, filled with water and a few apples

This used to be a carnival and Halloween favorite, but you don't see it as often today. Why not? It's still fun!

The premise is simple: Each person gets a turn of a specified amount of time (one minute is pretty fair) to try to pick an apple out of a pan of water, using only her/his teeth, no hands. If s/he succeeds, s/he gets to keep the apple. (If you wish, and you want to give the kids more incentive, you could award additional little prizes to each winner as well as the apple they know they could have gotten out of the fridge anyhow. Or let them play for the sheer fun of winning.)

After everyone has had a turn, everyone can have another turn, especially if there are still plenty of apples left. (You can put more than one apple per person into the pan—and don't expect everyone to get an apple within a minute, anyhow.)

This is fun for all ages—parents too, unless you wear false teeth!

DUNK TANK

Materials needed: Rubber ball or tennis ball, plastic wastebasket or pail filled part-way with water, chair that won't be ruined by getting wet, and three pieces of scrap lumber. Two pieces should be of equal length, and about four feet long, while the third should be narrow and at least three feet long

This one's only for good sports who are willing to take an unexpected shower! And it's definitely a warm-weather activity. Remember those carnival dunk tanks? By throwing a well-aimed ball, you could cause either a clown or, in the case of a charity carnival, a local celebrity to either be dunked into water or splashed with water. Here's your kids' chance to do the same to you— or each other.

A parent needs to prepare for this one by nailing the shorter, narrow piece of wood into one end of each of the two longer pieces of wood and then digging little holes and burying the other end of each of the longer pieces in the ground. You should now have something vaguely resembling a goal post. On top of the narrow crosspiece, balance the bucket full of water. More or less under the whole arrangement (you may have to experiment with position a little), place the chair, with the victim sitting in it.

Now each person gets three throws of the ball. Throw it at the wastebasket (hint: aim for the top), hoping to topple it and drench the victim underneath.

Be sure the wood posts are buried securely enough that the whole frame doesn't come toppling onto the victim at the first poorly aimed throw. Be sure the wastebasket is plastic, so if it hits the victim, no harm is done. Be sure the ball is lightweight for the same reason.

Kids just love getting Mom and Dad wet, but getting their siblings drenched is fun, too, so even if you aren't willing to participate, let the kids go ahead and try to "get" each other. The advantages of a dunk tank over a simple water pistol fight are the element of challenge— Can each person succeed in throwing well enough?— and the element of surprise: Neither the victim nor the pitcher knows in advance whether the throw will be a harmless dud or whether this will be the lucky pitch that sends the wastebasket full of water toppling, showering the victim.

Since everybody gets a turn under the bucket, and everybody gets three turns throwing per victim, everybody has a chance to get even—including Mom and Dad, if they want.

CARTON FORT/HOUSE/ SPACESHIP/CLUBHOUSE

Materials needed: Large carton (probably best found at an appliance store), scissors, possibly crayons or paints, lots of imagination

It's true that kids today are spoiled with electronic-this, mechanical-that, and automatic-the-other-thing. And it's true that some (not all) of these toys discourage, or at least fail to encourage, developing imaginations.

But maybe it's time to strike back. Give them something that is sure to encourage imaginative play. Like a box.

A box? Sure. Didn't you ever play spaceship or house or fort in an old refrigerator or stove or console-TV carton? Why deprive the kids of this experience? A big, sturdy carton can be anything they want it to be—a lunar landing module, a ranch bunkhouse—you name it.

Somebody—probably you—is going to have to cut out at least a door, and possibly windows if the kids want them and you're willing. (The door, at least, is necessary to get in and out.) From there, the kids can decorate the box with paints or crayons, drawing whatever suits the use to which they're putting the box.

Or, even better, don't paint it as a spaceship, and that way it can be a fort tomorrow and a school bus the next day.

Another great use for a big carton is as a clubhouse. Clubhouses lend themselves to all kinds of neat fun: Secret codes and passwords, club flags, meetings (with juice and cookies, of course), and agendas of Very Important Stuff to do.

And the next day, of course, the clubhouse can be a school/fort/jail/secret hiding place again.

COMMAND A FLEET

Materials needed: Paper, possibly paint or crayons

So you think you're too old to fly paper airplanes? Guess again! You can have as much fun as your kids designing and flying a fleet. Granted, coloring them with wild designs or realistically painting or crayoning them to look like jumbo jets may be more your kids' thing than yours. But folding them and flying them? Let go and be a kid again!

I could tell you a story about the people in a newspaper office who used to let off pressure after a deadline passed by taking old stationery, folding planes, and flying them at the other people's planes and at the people themselves.

But I won't tell you about the crew of crazies I once was in charge of. I'll tell you, instead, how to fold a very simple paper airplane, just in case you've left your childhood so far behind you that you've forgotten.

Holding a piece of paper in front of you in writing position—plain 8 ½″ × 11″ typing paper works fine—fold the two top corners down till what were the two sides of the top edge are touching each other at the midpoint of the page. Your page should now have an arrow-pointed top.

Now fold the two top sides inward again until what were the top right edge and top left edge are flush with the folded-over corners that are now in the middle of the page.

Last fold the two halves of the piece of paper back the other way at the midpoint, all the way down the page. Pull up the flaps and you have a rudimentary paper airplane. By experimenting with different kinds of folds and designs, as well as tearing tail flaps and adding paper clips for weights in one place or another, you can improve on the design so it flies farther, longer, and fancier.

Now your family can have contests: Whose plane flies the farthest? Whose can do the most or best tricks? You can have fights: Sail your planes at each other's planes, or even at each other, if you're respectful of other people's eyes.

WALNUT TOSS

Materials needed: Walnut, handful of washers tied
together with string, or any similar small, somewhat heavy object that will not roll far; also chalk
or several lengths of string

This game can be played indoors or out. The object is
to toss a projectile at a target on the ground or floor. The
small, weighty projectile you toss can be either of the
items suggested above or anything else around the house
that fits the general description and serves the purpose.
It should be compact, weighty enough to carry well, yet
not so heavy as to make the game difficult for any young
players in your family.

This game can be played indoors or out. If you play
on a sidewalk, driveway, or other paved surface, you
can draw your target with chalk. For play indoors, or
outdoors on grass, lay out your target with string: Cut
three lengths of string of unequal lengths. The first time
you play, try lengths of ten inches, twenty inches, and
thirty-five inches. Later you can adjust this in accordance
with your family members' ages and skill, making the
target larger or smaller as desired. Lay the smallest string
down in a circle and make two more circles around it
with the two other pieces of string. If using chalk on
pavement, draw a similar target with the chalk.

With chalk or another piece of string, draw a line
behind which everyone is to stand when tossing their
projectile. How far back from the target this is will
depend again on the ages and skill of your players. The
object, of course, is simply to toss your projectile onto
the target. Landing your projectile entirely within the
inner circle (bull's-eye) is worth 5 points. If it touches
any part of the middle circle, it's worth 3 points, whether
or not it's also touching the bull's-eye or the outer circle.

And if it's touching the outer circle but not the middle circle, whether or not it's entirely within the outer circle, it's worth 1 point.

The first player to accumulate 30 points wins.

If you find the game is taking too long and the players are getting restless, you'll know that next time you need to do one of three things: Move the throwing line nearer the target, make the circles larger, or make the winning score 25 or even 20 instead of 30. Conversely, if the players are winning too easily and quickly, you can do either of the three opposite things: Move the throwing line farther away from the target, make the circles smaller, or make the winning score higher so no one wins as easily.

STILS

Materials needed: Scrap lumber, nails

If you have a workshop in your home, and one of you—father, mother, or significantly older child—is even marginally handy at building things, it's easy to make stilts for your children to walk on. If you don't have pieces of wood that are the right size in your scrap pile, you can always visit a lumber yard and pick up what you need inexpensively, but chances are you may have something suitable among your discards.

A stilt is comprised of two pieces of wood. One long pole, which is square rather than round, and the little footrest that's attached to it. The height of the two stilts should be equal, and slightly taller than the shoulders of the child using them. Too tall and they're unwieldy; too short and the child can't get a secure grip on them. They need to be broad enough around to be sturdy, narrow enough that the child can get a good grip around them. Your child's age and size will dictate what's the best width. Make sure the handhold area is free of splinters.

The footrest can be rectangular or triangular in shape. If triangular, it should be a right triangle, with the top parallel to the ground. The footrest should be broad enough for a substantial portion of the child's foot to fit on. Using nails (or a glue you're very confident in), secure each footrest to one of the stilts. The footrests have to match in height but not appearance. One can actually be an odd triangular piece of wood you have lying around and the other an odd rectangular piece, so long as both are broad enough to support a good portion of the child's sole and both are attached to the stilt at approximately equal heights.

The height of the footrest will depend on the age and height of your child. It should be an easy step up from the ground for the child. Additionally, if the child has never used stilts before, start him/her out gently with only a slight elevation. The lower the stilt, the easier to control (and the less far the child will fall after the inevitable spills).

Of course, if the child is old enough, you can let him or her help you make the stilts instead of just watching, but the togetherness aspect of the stilts doesn't have to end with building them together. When's the last time you walked on stilts? Why not make a pair of stilts for every member of the family, parents included?

WATER, WATER EVERYWHERE

Materials needed: Large appliance box, garden hose, scissors or knife to cut a hole in the box

This is a game for a hot day. Sorry, you apartment dwellers will get left out of this one. Besides the materials above, it requires a backyard.

Maybe you haven't recently had a refrigerator, stove, or other large appliance delivered, but you might be able to get a box from one from your local appliance stores.

You, the parent, should lay the box on its side and cut a hole in the bottom of the box, about two feet in diameter. Leave the box on its side. Check first to be sure there are no staples or other hazards inside the box.

One or two kids or perhaps three if they're little, can play at a time. They enter the open top of the box while you turn the hose on and splash the box. It makes a wonderful racket the kids will love.

Now they can taunt you by emerging from the open end of the box or sticking their heads out the hole you cut in the bottom. When they do, you turn the hose on them, but being quick, they dive back into the safety of the box. Perhaps you'll manage to wet them first; perhaps you won't. It all depends on who's faster and on how daring they are.

Of course, you can cheat and spray into the box, forcing the kids to run out and around. But avoid spraying directly in their faces or with too hard a jet of water.

This is great fun for kids, especially those in the 3-to-8-year-old range.

Depending on how hard and long you play, the box may hold up for several days before it becomes too soggy and collapses.

BACKYARD CARNIVAL PITCHING GAMES

Materials needed: Rubber ball or tennis ball, and variously: wastebaskets, empty plastic milk jugs, empty soda cans

The kids can put on a carnival in which the whole family can participate, or they can simply have fun with any one of these games on a warm afternoon in the backyard.

If they do put on a carnival, it can be for just the family or something neighbors and friends are invited to participate in as well. The kids may really relish

playing the part of carnival barkers (complete with cur-
licue moustaches drawn on their upper lips with Mom's
eyeliner or eyebrow pencil, and a top hat if Dad has one
or if they can make one out of black construction paper),
or they may be too busy playing all the games to get into
the barker role.

If they do choose to make a whole production out of
the games and put on a carnival, other games in this
book that lend themselves to a carnival include "Hit
the Clown" (page 112), "Hungry Clown" (page 113),
"Marble Roll" (page 108), "Bobbing for Apples" (page
127), "Dunk Tank" (page 128), "Beanbag Toss" (page
125), and "Walnut Toss" (page 132).

Now, what about these pitching games?

1. Line up three wastebaskets in a row leading away
   from a starting line that's been drawn in the dirt,
   chalked on the driveway, or otherwise marked or
   decided upon (an imaginary line from a particular
   tree to the rosebushes, for instance). Each child gets
   five tosses of the ball and wins one point for landing
   the ball in the nearest wastebasket, two points for
   landing it in the middle wastebasket, and five points
   for landing it in the farthest wastebasket.

   For carnival play, each player can get a ticket (made
   of cut-up construction paper) with the number of points
   s/he won written on the ticket. For single-game play,
   the winner is the player who scored the greatest number
   of points with a set number of balls.

2. Stack up ten empty soda cans as follows: Four in a
   row on the bottom, three in a row on top of those
   four, two on top of the three, and one on top of
   the two. The players each have to stand behind an
   agreed-upon line and get three throws each to knock
   down all ten cans. (If this proves too easy or too
   difficult, move the starting line forward or back, or
   allow more or fewer throws per player.)

   For carnival play, anyone succeeding in knocking

over all ten cans with three throws gets a ticket good for five points. For individual game play, the winner is the player who is successful most often after everyone has had an equal number of turns. Or just do it for the fun of it without having a winner.

3. Stand one empty milk jug up at a distance and have the players stand behind a line and pitch the ball at the milk jug, trying to knock it over. If this proves too difficult, move the line nearer the milk jug. If it proves too easy, either move the line farther back or fill the milk-jug partway with beans, lentils, barley, or something similar.

    For carnival play, everyone who succeeds gets a ticket worth one point. For individual game play, the winner is the player who is successful most often after everyone has had an equal number of turns. Or just do it for the fun of it without having a winner.

4. Place a table in the backyard and a wastebasket on top of the table. Each player must get on his or her knees behind a line and try to throw the ball up into the wastebasket from that position.

    For carnival play, everyone who succeeds gets a ticket worth five points. For individual game play, the winner is the player who is successful most often after everyone has had an equal number of turns. Or just do it for the fun of it without having a winner.

You can invent other games involving pitching or throwing, knocking over objects, making baskets, or similar challenges.

You can even adapt the games to indoor play: Try to throw a bean into a glass from a reasonable distance, or throw a wadded-up piece of paper into a wastebasket that's been set high up on a piece of furniture, possibly throwing while you're down on your knees. Just look around the house to see what you have around that suggests a game to you. The only limits are the available materials and your own imagination.

✂ Arts and Crafts Projects

FISH BOWLS

Materials needed: Heavy white paper plates, plastic wrap, paints, glue, Goldfish crackers

Here's a use for a plateful of Goldfish crackers that doesn't involve eating them. If you combine the crackers and plates with plastic wrap, glue, and paints, you get hours of fun and displayable art.

Start by painting water on the inside of one plate. You can make whimsical waves, or shades of blue or blue-green, or add whitecaps. Now, if you wish, add a few items to make the seascape more interesting: a ship or two, old logs, seaweed, maybe even a mermaid. What you paint is your choice.

Now add the fish. Glue them in place; if you wish, you can even paint them in bright tropical-fish colors or turn them into whales or sharks with darker paint.

Cover the finished plate with a piece of plastic wrap, which can also be decorated to achieve a three-dimensional look.

EASTER EGG TREE

Materials needed: Eggs, paint or commercial Easter egg dyes, possibly glitter and/or gold or silver braid or trim and/or sequins and paste, small dead limb or branch from bush or small tree, small container of dirt or piece of Styrofoam, pin or needle, disinfectant

If there are Christmas trees for Christmas, why not an Easter egg tree for the Easter bunny to leave his baskets under (or just as a fun decoration)?

Pierce both ends of the eggs carefully and blow the contents out, preferably on a morning when somebody wanted scrambled eggs for breakfast so you don't waste the contents. Swish around a little disinfectant inside and rinse out carefully. Let the eggs dry.

Now decorate them, using paints or Easter egg dye, possibly adding sequins, glitter, gold or silver braid or trim, or all of the above, using paste or glue to attach them. Now add a little glue inside the hole at one end of each egg; and, for each egg, on a twig sticking out from the small tree or bush branch. Slip each egg over one twig, and you have an Easter egg tree.

Anchor the tree in either a small container of dirt or a piece of Styrofoam.

MAGAZINE BUTTERFLIES

Materials needed: Paper, pencil or pen, magazine to cut up, pipe cleaners

This project is a cinch to make, and kids love doing these. The finished product looks great hanging in windows. Here's how you do it:

First, draw a large butterfly pattern (or several, of

varying sizes) on a piece of paper. Then, trace the paper onto a brightly colored magazine picture (or ad), and cut out the butterfly along the line you've just traced. Now fan-fold the butterfly horizontally, and wrap a piece of pipe cleaner around the middle to hold it. Then spread the wings out. The ends of the pipe cleaner serve as antennae.

Since each one you cut out comes from a different picture, no two will be alike even if they're all the same size; but for variety, kids can cut butterflies of slightly different sizes as well.

SIMULATED MARBLE CARVINGS

Materials needed: Equal parts vermiculite and modeling plaster, water, cardboard box, knives or other sharp tools

With knives or other sharp tools in use, this is clearly an activity for older kids. They can make their own marblelike blocks for carving into animals, people, or whatever takes their fancy. All they have to do is mix equal parts of vermiculite and modeling plaster with just enough water to create a creamy mixture, then pour the mixture into a cardboard box and allow it to solidify.

After it's hardened, remove it from the box. Carefully carve the block with knives or other sharp tools and proudly display the finished result.

MAKE A TREE OUT OF NEWSPAPERS

Materials needed: Four to twelve sheets of newspaper, scissors, tape

This is a just-for-fun project. There's no practical purpose to the thing; it's just a fun project to create. (Though the kids, with their imaginations, may indeed think up a fun game involving their trees once they've finished making them.) If the recycling collection truck hasn't just picked up all your papers, you've probably got enough on hand for each kid to make his or her own tree (or even a whole forest).

To start, lay out between four and twelve single pages of newspaper in this manner: Lay out the first page, and overlap the top of the second page over the bottom of the first page by about three inches. Now roll up the paper loosely till about three inches of the second page are still exposed. Overlap the top of the third page over those three inches and resume rolling. Continue in this manner until you have all the pages loosely rolled up. Tape with any kind of tape at the middle and at one end, which will be the bottom of the tree.

With scissors, cut once from the other (top) end of the rolled-up papers down almost as far as the middle where the tape is. Now cut twice more, at approximately even intervals around the rolled-up papers, making all three cuts go equally far down the roll.

Grasp the innermost part of the roll and carefully pull until the paper spreads into a tree.

FABRIC LANDSCAPES

Materials needed: Felt squares or fabric scraps, fabric glue, heavy paper or cardboard

Fabric landscapes are easy to make, so kids can get in on the fun once they're old enough to cut something resembling a mountain, an ocean, the sun, etc. out of felt or material. Felt squares are the best medium to work with, but fabric scraps, solid-colored old clothes, or anything similar can be cut up and used as well.

Fabric landscapes add a decorative touch to any wall, and make great gifts for grandparents' birthdays; or the kids may elect to keep their own handiwork and display it proudly in their own rooms. Here's a project to keep the whole family busy, with a pile of felt or fabric in the middle of the table, and everyone gathered around the table, each working on his or her own landscape.

All you do is cut the felt or fabric in the shape you want and paste it down. You can paste it on cardboard, heavy paper, or even the little cardboard squares that pantyhose comes wrapped around.

Overlap a fish on the water, the top of a tree over the sky, the tree's trunk over the green grass. Here are some tips from a professional artist, which the older and more proficient landscape-makers in the family can use to help make their fabric landscapes as good-looking as possible:

- Use the glue sparingly.
- Work from background to foreground.
  Make the sky and water the same color, but not necessarily blue. Yellow, pink, and violet work especially well. Or try black for a nighttime picture.
- Shade the mountains: Decide where the light source is, and use lighter tones of fabric on the light side of the mountains, darker tones on the shaded side. Remember, even snow has shadows, so if your mountains are snow-capped, use both white and beige fabrics to create shadows.
- Build groups of trees in layers, with lighter colors to the back. In landscapes, everything gets darker and bolder as it reaches the foreground. Gray or light blue are especially good colors for background trees because they create a misty effect. And trees in the far distance can be shaped only vaguely. In the background, you're creating the illusion of trees, rather than clearly defined trees themselves.
- Rocks are just small mountains, so shade them in the same way.

- Make a reflection in the water. Make the same shape of mountain or tree or groups of trees, but place them upside down.
- Where the water and shoreline meet, put a very thin strip of white or very light-colored fabric.

GOOD IMPRESSIONS

Materials needed: 1 cup of flour, ½ cup of salt, ½ cup of water. Optional: Paint

The kids can make plaques from impressions of their hands, and isn't that a lovely gift for Grandma's and Grandpa's birthdays, or for Grandparents' Day, or just as an I Love You present?

Here is how your child goes about making a handprint: S/he mixes the flour and salt together, adding the water gradually until the consistency is like clay. (A little less than the ½ cup may be sufficient.) After kneading it for about five minutes, it will be ready to use.

Now your child takes a ball of the clay, flattens it, and makes an impression of his/her hand in it. (Lightly flouring his/her hand first will help to keep it from sticking.) Your child can use a finger to sign his/her name below the handprint.

A larger ball of clay will accommodate two or three small hands, so the kids can all make their handprints at once, or each can do an individual plaque.

Plaques don't have to be limited to handprints. A leaf can delicately be pressed into clay to make an impression in it, as can various other items. Use your collective imaginations.

The edges of the flattened ball of clay can be smoothed out for a more finished look or left rough-looking for a more handmade look. Either way, you may want to punch a hole at the top so Grandma (or whoever is the recipient) can put a nail through the hole to hang the plaque.

The plaque needs to dry in the open air, preferably on a cake rack, for two days, or longer in a humid climate. Then it can be painted, if desired, and is ready to be given as a gift or hung in the child's own room.

CRAYON STAINED GLASS

Materials needed: Old crayons, newspapers, grater, waxed paper, Scotch tape, iron. Optional: Black construction paper

Here's a great use for stubs of nearly gone crayons (though you can certainly use crayons that aren't on their last legs if you wish). This project is definitely one for you to work on with the kids, since it involves the use of a grater and an iron. Here's how you proceed:

Tear the paper labels off the crayons, then grate them, letting all the different colors mix together. Put five layers of newspaper on your ironing board and set the iron on low (dry, not steam). On top of the newspaper, place one square of waxed paper. The size is up to you, but about a foot square is a good choice. Place the crayon gratings on the waxed paper; don't clump them too thickly, as you'll be surprised at how well they cover, once they melt. Now put a second square of waxed paper on top of the brightly colored crayon shavings.

With your iron still on low, iron the waxed paper until all the crayon gratings melt and run together. After your stained glass panel has cooled, tape it to a window and admire its jewellike glow in the light.

Optional: To create the appearance of a cathedral window, cut symmetrical designs in a piece of black construction paper, tape your stained glass panel to the construction paper, then mount the whole thing on a window.

This activity is great for anyone, but especially for

kids who feel left behind by their siblings or friends with more artistic ability. They can create beautiful stained glass designs even if they can't draw a straight line or a recognizable dog or cat.

GET SOME LONG LITTLE DOGGIES

Materials needed: Empty cardboard toilet paper tubes, construction paper or plain typing paper, crayons, pipe cleaners, tape, scissors

Using the cardboard tube as the body and pipe cleaners as legs and the tail, even very small kids can make a whole family of pups whose only limit will be the supply of empty rolls. Very small kids may need an adult's help to punch the small holes into which the legs are inserted.

If your toilet paper comes on brown cardboard rolls, great; if not, crayons will soon make the roll dog-colored, or don't strive for a dachshund look in particular, and color the dog any way you wish. Since these are fantasy pups, there's nothing to stop them from having dachshunds' bodies with dalmatians' spots.

One pipe cleaner can be inserted through two close-together holes at the rear to make the two back legs, with the process repeated in front for the front legs. Or forget about the dogs being dachshunds and give them longer legs composed of one pipe cleaner each.

The pipe cleaner tail can be inserted into the top of the rear of the tube, or a piece of paper can be taped over the open end and the tail inserted through the paper. Or as a tail-wagging variation, instead of using a pipe cleaner, accordion-fold an oblong of construction paper a quarter inch wide by four inches long and tape it on. This tail will wag by itself in a breeze or if the dog is moved.

If the pipe cleaner tail and limbs are simply inserted through holes in the tube, they can be reinforced with tape.

Draw the head on paper, then connect it to the body by a pipe cleaner neck, or tape it directly to the roll.

These dogs won't shake hands or play tricks, but they also won't chase cars or dig up your daffodils!

NATURE'S WRAPPING PAPER

Materials needed: Butcher paper, newspaper (to protect work surface), tape, leaves and/or flowers and/or ferns, tempera paint, toothbrush or other stiff-bristled brush, window screening

A small version of this project can be framed and hung, but its basic use is as wrapping paper, and wouldn't it make a great wrap for Grandma's or Grandpa's birthday present?

Start outdoors by gathering leaves and/or flowers and/or ferns. Vary what you pick in size and shape; color is irrelevant. Now, back indoors, spread out newspaper to cover your work surface, and then tape the butcher paper to the newspaper. Arrange the greenery on the butcher paper without a whole lot of overlapping, hold the screening over the paper, and dip the brush in the tempera. Rub the brush across the screening, allowing the paint to splatter onto the paper in a fine mist. You can splatter all one color of paint, or vary the effect by using two or even more colors.

When the paint is dry, remove the greenery, which can be discarded or reused for more wrapping paper.

BLOTTOS

Materials needed: Paper, watercolor or thin tempera paint, scissors, paste

You never know what you'll end up with when you start making Blottos, but you can be sure of one thing: You'll have fun doing it.

Cut pieces of paper to various sizes, creasing each piece in the middle so that, later, it can easily be folded over. Then sprinkle just a few small drops of paint on one side of the crease and fold the paper on the creased line with the paint inside. This causes the paint to be squeezed into interesting shapes.

When you open the paper, you'll be surprised to find what the paint has turned into. Your resultant design may look like an insect, a flower, an animal, or a mythical creature.

After you've created several Blotto designs, cut them each out and glue them onto a piece of construction paper to create a picture, which may look like abstract art or may actually look like something, but either way is bound to be interesting.

PUSSYWILLOW SERENADE

Materials needed: Pussywillow buds; construction paper or typing paper (construction paper, being heavier, is preferable); pencil, crayons, or markers

Surely your child has seen comic book or cartoon pictures of cats—solo or in multiples—sitting on a fence and serenading the neighborhood with a chorus of meows. If s/he's a reasonably proficient artist, have her/him draw a fence; if not, you do it. Now s/he can glue the pussywillows to the paper so that the furry grey buds are sitting right on top of the line of the fence.

(Time out while s/he—and you—stroke the pussywillow buds and admire their furry softness.)

Now s/he draws heads and/or ears, and tails, on the paper onto which the pussywillows are glued, completing the picture of the backs of cats sitting on a fence. Now all that's missing is a cartoon-style balloon for each cat, with "Meow" coming out of it. (Or "Mrrowrr," or whatever your child thinks transcribes a cat's utterances.)

Just don't throw shoes at the picture.

HANDPRINT TULIPS

Materials needed: Fingerpaints, paints, paper, soap and water

The concept for this one is really simple: The child spreads fingerpaint over the palm side of his or her entire hand—fingers and all—and, with fingers slightly (not widely) spread, imprints the paper about midway down, near the edge of the paper. Then, after washing the paint off, s/he applies a different color and does the same thing about an inch away. If there's room for a third handprint, do it in another color. The handprints all represent tulips, and the colors chosen should be suitable for that flower—red, yellow, and deep purple are good choices.

After washing his/her hands again, the child turns to the regular paint and, using green paint and a brush, the child draws a stem beneath each tulip, and a little grass growing below.

How does your garden grow?

PLASTIC MASKS

Materials needed: Gallon-size plastic containers, elastic string (to hold the masks on). Optional: Pipe cleaners, feathers, sequins, paint, yarn, paper, glue or paste

Empty gallon-size plastic containers make great masks, and they're durable. Carefully cut the containers in half, then cut out openings for eyes, nose, and mouth. A piece of elastic string will hold the mask in place.

A white or opaque container by itself is a great ghost mask. For something more creative, use any of the optional materials listed above or be creative and come up with your own materials, gluing or pasting them in place. Pipe cleaners can make a moustache or eyebrows, as can crepe paper or yarn. Sequins or feathers will give an exotic look. Yarn makes hair. Be creative. Be outrageous! Let yourself go.

SYRUP PAINTINGS

Materials needed: Heavy paper plate, marker, Karo syrup, food coloring, paper cup(s), paint-brush(es)

Has this ever happened to you? It's a rainy weekend, the kids are bored; they finally decide they want to paint, but you find you're all out of paint, and you don't feel like going to the store in the rain. Have I just described a glum scenario? If you have the ingredients listed above, you're not in such bad shape after all. Here's what the kids (and you too—c'mon, it's fun!) can do:

Stir a drop or two of food coloring into a paper cup

full of Karo syrup. Repeat the process for each color you want to use. Now, using a marker, draw a design on a heavy paper plate, then paint the design with the syrup paint. You can draw a realistic picture or an intricate geometric design or a bit of abstract art. You can work all in one color or use several.

An ordinary paintbrush works fine for this, though you have to be extra careful washing it.

Let the picture dry on a flat surface; it takes about twenty-four hours. Now it's ready to be hung and admired.

PAPIER-MACHE MARACAS

Materials needed: Old burned-out lightbulbs; newspapers, paper toweling, or any other absorbent paper; scissors; paste thinned to the consistency of cream; large container for mixing the paste; Vaseline; sandpaper; paint (tempera, latex, or enamel); paintbrush; clear plastic shellac or varnish, if tempera paint is used

This one's for somewhat older kids since there's broken glass inside the maracas. The maracas shouldn't break apart if used properly, but little kids might decide to take the maracas apart to see what makes them rattle. Really young ones are too young to construct these maracas themselves, anyhow, so best leave this project for the older kids.

This is a great way to recycle burned-out lightbulbs into something fun. The kids can spend a part of an evening on the project; why not serve them guacamole or nachos, play Latin music on the radio if you live in an area that has a Spanish station, play the maracas after you've made them, and turn the whole evening into a fiesta!

Here's how to make the maracas:

Cover the lightbulb with a thin coat of Vaseline. Cut the paper into strips about eight to twelve inches long and about an inch to an inch and a half wide. If you haven't already thinned the paste to the consistency of cream, do so now.

Dip the paper strips into the paste, wipe off the excess paste, and apply the paper directly to the coated surface of the bulb. Continue applying paper until you've added six layers of paper to the bulb. Apply each of the layers in a different direction, to make the finished product stronger. Be sure all the wrinkles are out.

Allow the maracas to dry, then rap them against the floor to break the light bulb inside the paper covering of each. The broken glass will provide the rattling sound of the maracas. You, the parent, should at this point check carefully for any gaps in the paper through which broken glass might leak out. If there are any such leaks, repair them with additional strips of paste-saturated paper.

Sand the surface until smooth, and paint. If desired, and especially if you've used tempera paint, which tends to smear, spray with shellac or varnish. You now have maracas.

ICKY WITCH

Materials needed: Egg carton, markers or construction paper, glue, scissors, yarn or weeds

You, too, can have a witch of your very own—and an icky-looking one, too. Just as icky as you want to make her. Or should I say, "them," since from each egg carton you can make three witches. It's simple—just cut the top off an egg carton, then cut the bottom into three sets of four cups. Each set will be the basis of one witch's face.

For each witch, make the top two cups (it doesn't matter which way you hold the four-cup set) into two eyes by drawing with markers or by gluing circles of colored paper into the bottom of the cups. If your egg carton is made of Styrofoam, the marker may not adhere, and construction paper is the way to go. If your egg carton is made of cardboard, the choice is yours.

The bump sticking up between the cups is the witch's nose; you can draw two dots for nostrils with a marker if you wish. Draw a line connecting the bottom two cups to make a mouth out of them, or glue construction paper on. The mouth can smile or frown as you wish.

Yarn or dried weeds make great hair. If desired, you can even spray the weeds with spray paint, but actually, natural dried weed color is a great hair color for an icky witch.

Hang your witch on a wall, or leave it on your night table or dresser as a decoration. Use it as a centerpiece at a Halloween party, or make several witches and put on a puppet show.

KISSY-FACE PICTURES

Materials needed: Lipstick; paper (white or pale construction paper, typing paper, or other unlined writing paper); old magazines, scissors, and paste or glue; or crayons or colored markers

I know, I know. This is supposed to be a book of fun for the whole family, yet this particular project clearly leaves out the boys and the daddies. They certainly won't want any part of an activity that starts with putting on lipstick! But there are families with only girls, no boys, and with only one parent, Mommy. So for them, this is an all-family project. And there's no reason why, for the rest of you, part of the family can't enjoy making kissy-face pictures.

As I said, it's a project that sanctions your daughter putting on Mommy's lipstick. The result is a picture that can be completed either of two ways. Here's how she proceeds:

Put on lipstick, then kiss the paper about two-thirds of the way down, making a firm impression and holding still, so as not to smudge. You now have the mouth of the face you're going to create. Now cut out eyes, nose, eyebrows, hair, and possibly ears from pictures in magazines. It's more fun if you cut them all out of different pictures (but not the two eyes out of two different pictures!). Glue or paste the various features in appropriate places in relation to the kissy-lips.

Or just draw in the features with crayons or markers.

For variety, try kissing several different pieces of paper with your mouth set a different way each time: closed, open, smiling, pouting, or sadly turned down. In the open-mouthed picture, you can add a tongue and teeth, and possibly even words coming out of the mouth in a cartoon-style balloon.

SALT-AND-FLOUR BEADS

Materials: 2 cups of table salt, 1 cup of flour, water, food coloring or paint (acrylic or tempera)

Mix the salt and flour with enough water to make a doughy mixture. If desired, add food coloring. Form small pieces of the mixture into dough. Pierce each piece with a toothpick and let it dry.

When all the pieces are formed and dried, if you didn't color them with food coloring, you can paint them with tempera or acrylic paints. String them into necklaces, bracelets, or rings; or you can make them large and shape them around soda straws for macramé.

Now, proudly show off your new jewelry.

STUFFED PAPER FISH

Materials needed: Large sheets of butcher paper, staples, paint and brush, newspaper, string

Your kids may want a whole school of these delightful fish hanging from the ceiling in their rooms, and unless your kids are really little, they can do it all themselves. Here's how:

Hold two pieces of butcher paper together and cut a fish design out. If cutting both at once is too difficult for the children, they can trace the same design on two different sheets of paper, then cut each one, one at a time.

Staple the outside edges together, leaving about a five-inch opening. Through that opening, carefully stuff the fish with small pieces of newspaper that have been crumpled up. When you're through stuffing them, staple the fish closed the rest of the way.

Finally, paint the fish, remembering scales and gills. Paint something relatively tame like goldfish, something brighter and wilder like assorted tropicals, or go all out and create wild designs never known on any fish yet seen. Hang them from your ceiling on strings.

With these fish, you don't even have to remember to feed them and change the water.

POTATO-PRINT WRAPPING PAPER

Materials needed: Medium to large baking potato; sharp knife; ink pad (preferably with colored ink), or as an alternative, paper towel with slightly diluted food color (in lieu of ink); large sheets of paper from a drawing pad

Involving sharp knives, this activity is only for children old enough to use knives responsibly. Since the carving is an integral part of the process and the fun, it's not suggested that younger kids take part in this activity, with you, the parent, doing the carving.

With this activity, the child has not only the pleasure of designing an artistic sculpture but also of creating custom made wrapping paper that features the child's own design. Here's how s/he proceeds:

Cut the potato in half. Carve your own design (pattern, random design, simple picture, newly invented family crest, initials, or whatever) onto the cut end of one potato half. Remember that if you carve a letter (other than *A, H, I, M, O, T, U, V, W,* or *X*), you need to carve it backward for the stamp to print the right way.

You'll be most successful if you arrange for your design to stick up rather than to be cut down into the potato. In other words, if you want to make an *X*, don't dig an *X* shape into the potato, but rather cut away all the parts around the *X* shape, leaving the *X* sticking up.

Ink the carved potato using the stamp pad (or a paper towel, stashed safely in a bowl and soaked with food coloring). Using your personally designed potato as you would any stamp pad, stamp the design all over the paper, reinking as necessary.

Bonus: If you fold a piece of paper in quarters, you can use your customized potato stamp designs to personalize the paper into instant stationery.

MIRROR-DESIGN NAME

Materials needed: Two sheets of construction paper of different colors, pencil, scissors, glue

Since each child in your family has a different name, each child is going to wind up with a different pattern by following the same instructions, below:

Fold a sheet of construction paper in half lengthwise. Write your name in outline letters, with the bottoms of the letters resting on the folded edge. Carefully cut out your name, being careful not to cut the portion of the letters that rests on the fold.

Unfold the paper, and you'll see your name and a mirror image of it as well. Glue the name to a second sheet of construction paper. Use a pen or crayons to add color and pizzazz to your design.

If you hold it at arms' length and squint, you may envision animals, a totem pole, or whatever your imagination can conjure up.

Parents, if you've given up on fitting all that wonderful artwork on the limited space on your fridge door, consider devoting a portion of a hallway wall or family room wall to taped-up masterpieces by your budding artists. And if you do decide to do this, what better way is there to show which section of the wall belongs to which young artist than by delineating their respective sections by hanging these mirror-design names at the top of each child's section of the wall.

CHALK-AND-STENCIL WALL HANGINGS

Materials needed: Heavy paper, colored chalk, heavy textured paper, tissue

These wall hangings are so beautiful that no one would ever guess just how easy they are to make. Start by cutting a stencil from heavy paper. Good shapes to begin with include butterflies, flowers, and leaf or fern designs.

Outline the edges of the stencil with colored chalk, then lay the stencil carefully on a piece of heavy, textured paper and use a soft tissue to wipe the chalk from the stencil onto the paper. This produces a very soft, subtle effect.

Remove the stencil from the paper, apply a different color of chalk to the edges, and reposition the stencil on the paper, changing the orientation slightly, too. Now

repeat the wiping process. Try to use related colors—
different shades of blue, for example—and remember to
overlap a few of the outlines.

SODA-AND-CORNSTARCH MODELING

Materials needed: 1 cup cornstarch, 2 cups baking soda, 1 ¼ cups water, food coloring

You can make your own low-cost mixture for modeling
out of the ingredients above. Just mix the cornstarch, soda,
and water in a large saucepan and cook over medium heat
until the mixture has thickened to a doughy consistency.
Then turn it out onto a breadboard or a piece of waxed
paper or foil.

After it has cooled slightly, knead food coloring into
the dough. It's now ready to be modeled into whatever
your kids want to turn it into. Excess mixture, to be saved
for another day, should be stored in the refrigerator in a
plastic bag to keep it soft.

Kids (other than the really young ones) can even
do the preparation themselves, adding to their pride in
craftsmanship.

GESSO PLATE

Materials needed: Commercial dry-ground gesso;
paper plates; shellac, varnish, or clear plastic
spray; brush; tempera or enamel paint

These plates make wonderful gifts for Grandma, a
favorite aunt, or the neighbor who always has cookies
or other treats for your kids. They're beautiful, they're
sturdy, and they're functional, too.

Mix the gesso according to the directions on the can
until it's the consistency of heavy cream. Next, paint
two or three paper plates with the gesso and press the

plates together while wet. Make sure the edges fit tightly. Continue applying the gesso until the cracks or nicks are all filled or until the plate is as thick as you want it to be. Then sandpaper the plate until it's smooth, and paint the entire plate. Finally, decorate it with additional paint, and apply one or two coats of shellac, varnish, or clear plastic spray.

BREAD-DOUGH CLAY

Materials needed: 4 slices of bread, 3 tablespoons of white glue, 2 drops of lemon juice, paint and brush

After removing the crusts, tear the bread into small pieces, then mix with the glue and lemon juice. Use the mixture to form animals, flowers, or whatever. Allow it to dry for one or two days before painting.

Excess clay can be stored in a plastic bag in the refrigerator for use another day.

HOMEMADE FINGER PAINT

Materials needed: ½ cup soap chips, 6 cups water, 1 cup liquid starch, food coloring

What could be more economical than to save money on items the kids love to play with, which cost you money repeatedly at the store? Take finger paints. If your family is like many others, you probably go through lots of this commodity, and after a while the cost adds up. Here's your chance to save money by making your own finger paints. The kids can even help you. They may enjoy making the finger paints as much as they enjoy using them.

Dissolve the soap in three cups of water until the mixture is smooth. Then blend in the starch and the other three cups of water. Pour into as many different containers as you want colors, and add food coloring a little at a time until you get to the desired shade.

Your kids are now ready to have fun, and when they say, "I did it myself," they'll really mean it. They did it all from scratch.

CUSTOM-DESIGNED PRINTING ROLLER

Materials needed: Thick felt or yarn, heavy cardboard wrapping paper tube, painting roller, paint, paper

Cut a heavy cardboard wrapping paper tube to the length of a painting roller. Glue pieces of thick felt or yarn onto the tube. The kids can experiment with different configurations of felt or yarn to get different designs on different tubes.

Slip the tube over the painting roller and roll the roller in paint; then roll it over a piece of paper. The result will be abstract art in unique designs. This one's great for kids with ten thumbs who want to create some pretty art but who can't even draw a recognizable stick figure.

TIE-DYED PAPER TOWELS

Materials needed: Plain white paper towels, food coloring, one bowl for each color used (or a muffin tin, with different colors in different cups), water

You may think of tie-dyeing in terms of T-shirts, not paper towels, but the colorful oblongs that result from this activity have their purpose: Your kids can hang the colored paper towels on a string, like flags, to decorate their rooms, or they can tape them to their windows, letting the sun shine through them. Girls may want to use them as bedspreads for doll houses. The kids can even wrap small presents in them. As a wrapping paper, they're both unique and inexpensive.

Unlike the process for tie-dyeing shirts, the paper towels shouldn't be crumpled or rubber-banded; simply fold them. (Let your kids decide what pattern of folds suits them best.) They can fold the towel any number of times and at weird angles.

The dye is actually food coloring mixed with water. By using different dilutions, you can make several different shades out of the same color. You can also make a third color by mixing two or more colors together.

The idea isn't to dunk the whole towel into the bowl or muffin tin cup, but rather to submerge this corner and that into the bowl, wetting specific areas. The kids can even dunk the same folded towel into more than one cup, getting more than one color on it. This can be different shades of the same color, such as red, deep rose, and light pink, or complementary colors, such as blue and violet, or even contrasting colors, as red and yellow.

When each towel is unfolded, a completely unique and interesting pattern of color will appear like magic on what had been a plain piece of blank white paper a few minutes before.

You may want to spread out some newspaper as a good surface for the paper towels to dry on, to avoid getting dye where it will be hard to remove later.

PATTERNED SCARECROW

Materials needed: Outdated wallpaper sample book (ask your local wallpaper or interior decorating store for a discard), scissors, construction paper or cardboard from cardboard box, glue or paste, patterns (to be made by parent). Optional: Straw, dried grass, or straw-colored yarn

You, the parent, should probably make the patterns (out of newspaper, construction paper, or typing paper)

for the shirt, pants, and hat of a comical scarecrow in the *Wizard of Oz* tradition. Your children can then go through the samples of wallpaper to choose which patterns s/he'll want to use for the pants, shirts, and hats of the several scarecrows they'll probably each create.

The kids place the patterns on the wallpaper samples, trace the patterns carefully, then cut out the pieces. The scarecrows themselves will be cut out of cardboard or construction paper. The kids can then glue the clothes to the scarecrows. (Each child will probably want to make several different scarecrows, each with different patterns.)

The scarecrows' faces should be drawn on white paper, then glued to the cardboard or construction paper head.

If desired, the kids can glue straw, dried grass, or straw-colored yarn at the ends of the sleeves and pants-legs, for an even more realistic appearance.

These scarecrows may not ward off the predators in your vegetable garden, but they're charming and cheery to have around, and a fun project for a rainy day.

EGG CARTON CATERPILLARS

Materials needed: Egg carton(s); scissors; paint, crayons, or markers. Optional: Pipe cleaners, glue, construction paper, yarn, googly eyes (from a crafts store)

Here's one caterpillar that won't imperil your vegetable garden, and the kids will have fun making it. By cutting an egg carton in half lengthwise, they'll wind up with two unimpressive rows of six cups each. But if they turn either half over, they've now got six humps— and the beginning of a caterpillar.

The most basic caterpillar can be made by coloring or painting the half-carton green (or brown, or even some other color if the kids want a fantastic, not-to-be-confused-with-reality caterpillar). Then they draw or paint eyes and a mouth at the front. (Which end is the front? You'd have to ask the caterpillar.)

A couple of fuzzy antennae can be made by sticking lengths of pipe cleaner from the top of the head or face. Do the kids want them curly, straight, twisted? Depends what kind of a caterpillar they're creating.

These caterpillars can be as elaborate and varied as desired. Glue googly eyes to the head instead of coloring in the eyes, for a comical effect. Yarn hair, even eyebrows or moustaches can personalize the caterpillar until no butterfly or moth would recognize it as a possible offspring, but anyone would recognize it as cute.

Outfit the caterpillar. How about a top hat made out of construction paper? How about a construction-paper cane for every leg? Have a mile of inch-worm fun!

ENHANCE FAMILY LIFE

__MOMMY, THERE'S NOTHING TO DO!__
   Cynthia MacGregor   0-425-13911-5/$4.50
A collection of easy ideas children can enjoy with
parents or alone on rainy days, long trips, or any time.

*Don't miss these Cynthia MacGregor
titles for even more family entertainment...*

__FREE* FAMILY FUN__ *(AND SUPER CHEAP)
                           0-425-14367-8/$4.50
__TOTALLY TERRIFIC FAMILY GAMES__
                           0-425-14574-3/$4.99

__THE HOMEWORK PLAN__
   Linda Sonna, Ph.D.   0-425-14499-2/$4.99
**"A homework survival handbook for busy
parents..."**—*Positive Parenting* magazine
Education expert and psychologist Linda Sonna
reveals simple methods to enrich communication
and improve your child's performance.

__STRESS STRATEGIES FOR PARENTS__
   Kimberly Barrett, Ph.D.   0-425-13626-4/$4.99
Dr. Barrett offers busy parents smart strategies to help
them handle stress...and handle their children with the
right mix of attention, discipline and love.

Payable in U.S. funds. No cash orders accepted. Postage & handling: $1.75 for one book, 75¢
for each additional. Maximum postage $5.50. Prices, postage and handling charges may
change without notice. Visa, Amex, MasterCard call 1-800-788-6262, ext. 1, refer to ad # 537

Or, check above books and send this order form to: The Berkley Publishing Group 390 Murray Hill Pkwy., Dept. B East Rutherford, NJ 07073	Bill my: ☐ Visa ☐ MasterCard ☐ Amex
	Card#_____ (expires)
	Signature_____ ($15 minimum)
Please allow 6 weeks for delivery.	Or enclosed is my: ☐ check ☐ money order
Name_____	Book Total $_____
Address_____	Postage & Handling $_____
City_____	Applicable Sales Tax $_____
State/ZIP_____	(NY, NJ, PA, CA, GST Can.) Total Amount Due $_____

FOR YOU AND YOUR TODDLER

__**GOOD-BYE DIAPERS** *Batya Swift Yasgur*
0-425-14185-3/$4.50

The parents' guide to successful, stress-free toilet training. *Good-bye Diapers* presents a variety of new techniques, enabling you to specifically design your child a complete toilet training program. Includes chapters on toilet training an older child, a one-day intensive program, and defining and preventing bedwetting.

__**TIME-OUT FOR TODDLERS**
  Dr. James W. Varni and Donna G. Corwin
  0-425-12943-8/$8.00

This guide illustrates the revolutionary TIME-OUT method that benefits both child and parent, showing parents how to cope with common childhood behaviors—such as temper tantrums, sibling rivalry, whining, and selfishness—in a positive and effective manner.

__**FOODS FOR HEALTHY KIDS**
  Dr. Lendon Smith 0-425-09276-3/$4.99

Dr. Lendon Smith, America's leading authority on nutrition for children, tells how to prevent and alleviate health problems such as asthma, allergies, depression, constipation, hyperactivity, sleep problems and tension—not with medicine, but with good, nourishing food. He gives you his total nutrition program, complete with more than 100 recipes.